# Public Personnel Administration and Constitutional Values

# Public Personnel Administration and Constitutional Values

*YONG S. LEE*

# Q

**QUORUM BOOKS**
WESTPORT, CONNECTICUT • LONDON

**Library of Congress Cataloging-in-Publication Data**

Lee, Yong S.
    Public personnel administration and constitutional values / Yong
S. Lee.
        p.  cm.
    Includes bibliographical references and index.
    ISBN 0–89930–610–1 (alk. paper)
        1. United States—Officials and employees.  2. United States—
Constitutional law.  3. Civil service—United States—Personnel
management.  I. Title.
    KF5337.L42  1992
    342.73′068—dc20
    [347.30268]      92–8404

British Library Cataloguing in Publication Data is available.

Library of Congress Catalog Card Number: 92–8404
ISBN: 0–89930–610–1

First published in 1992

Quorum Books, 88 Post Road West, Westport, CT 06881
An imprint of Greenwood Publishing Group, Inc.

Printed in the United States of America

The paper used in this book complies with the
Permanent Paper Standard issued by the National
Information Standards Organization (Z39.48–1984).

10 9 8 7 6 5 4 3 2 1

# *Contents*

# *Preface*

In the past, much of American scholarship in public personnel administration has focused primarily on what may be described as the science of personnel administration and relatively little on constitutional principles that define administrative behavior. This has created a rather large gap in the literature, as well as in administrative training. This book is an attempt to fill part of that gap.

Today, it is urgent that the discipline of public administration address that gap. This is because during the last three decades, the judiciary has fundamentally altered the relationship between public employment and the Constitution, bringing the employment relationship within the constitutional framework. Under the new framework, public administrators are required to manage personnel in a manner that is consistent with the Constitution. An effective administrator under this framework, therefore, must be competent not only in management skills but also in the knowledge of the established constitutional principles.

*Public Personnel Administration and Constitutional Values* examines the development and application of constitutional principles that underpin today's personnel administration in the United States. In particular, the text focuses on the case principles that bear upon critical personnel decisions—the decisions that affect disciplinary action, layoffs, affirmative action, promotion, compensation, and job termination. It addresses the bottom line of the employment relationship: what public administrators may or may not do lawfully in personnel management. To that end it reviews key court decisions, summarizes case principles, and explores their implications for policy and management.

The theme of this book is that the basic personnel principles in American public administration are not founded in the concept of managerial efficiency—although many classical writers tried to make a case for it—but rightfully have roots in the Constitution. What ultimately matters, therefore, is the Constitution, and how the courts interpret it as it pertains to public personnel administration. Thus, the controversial personnel decisions that touch upon basic constitutional values are to be resolved ultimately by the judiciary—although not always. And the views from the bench set forth the basic ground rules for personnel policy and administration.

In preparing this text I have had three specific audiences in mind. The first audience is the students of public administration in the United States. The text is designed to underscore the centrality of constitutional values in the study of personnel administration. The emphasis on constitutional values is a newer tradition emerging in contemporary public administration. The second audience is the practitioners of public management, whether they are in supervisory positions or in subordinate roles, personnel administrators or general administrators, public or private. The cases that are reviewed and the managerial implications explored in this text should be of value to those who have little time to wade through volumes of court cases searching for the established constitutional principles.

The third audience is the students of personnel administration in other parts of the world. The personnel principles introduced in this text can be seen as an expression of American constitutional values and ideals—principally in pursuit of human freedom, liberty, and fairness in employment. People in many parts of the world today are still struggling to overcome prejudice, discrimination, and mistreatment for reasons of race, color, religion, sex, and national origin. I am confident that the American experience shall provide them with a rare insight.

## THE ORGANIZATION OF THE CHAPTERS

The chapters that follow in this book are organized around case law principles that are central to critical public decision making, principles that affect and relate to hiring, termination, promotion, compensation, layoffs, and affirmative action. Each chapter looks at the development of case law and identifies key issues. This is not a book on constitutional law. Also, various topics within personnel management are not treated comprehensively. The purpose of the chapters is to provide a glimpse at the emerging public management environment that is grounded in the Constitution.

Chapters 2 and 3 focus on the relationship between public employment and the Constitution. In particular, chapter 2 reviews the public employment relationship within the context of the Due Process Clause, and chapter 3 examines the relationship in the context of First Amendment freedoms. The central problem of constitutional law regarding First Amendment freedoms is to find an equilibrium between the need of a public employee, as a citizen, to exercise his or her rights and the need of government to restrict such exercises.

Chapters 4 and 5 look at the evolution of the Equal Protection Clause as it relates to employment discrimination and remedial affirmative action. Chapter 4 focuses on the legal theory of discrimination under Title VII, including the disparate treatment approach and the disparate impact approach. To raise a prima facie case of discrimination based on race or gender, the employee must carry the burden of proving that he or she has been unlawfully discriminated against by his or her employer. Legal technicalities abound in the construction of a prima facie case of discrimination. A major controversy surrounding the legal theory of discrimination is the allocation of evidentiary burdens. Affirmative action represents the other side of the same coin, in which the employer carries the burden of proving that the remedial action taken remains within the bounds of the Constitution and Title VII. Chapter 5 examines the review standards the courts use to determine the validity of affirmative action decisions.

Discrimination in compensation on the basis of gender is a special controversy arising from Title VII. The controversy in recent years has been unnecessarily limited to a debate on comparable worth. Chapter 6 explores a broader Title VII approach to gender discrimination in pay, including claims based on unequal pay for equal work, unjustified pay disparity for those who are similarly situated, and unequal pay for comparable worth. To seek clarification of case law affecting these claims, the chapter examines how lower federal courts actually respond to gender-based wage discrimination claims.

Chapter 7 looks at the development of case law dealing with governmental and official liability involving civil damages. In particular, the chapter examines the circumstances under which governmental entities and public officials (in their personal capacity) may be held liable in civil suits. The chapter also examines the characteristics of lawsuits litigated in federal district courts.

# Acknowledgments

This book grew out of a graduate seminar on public personnel administration that I taught at Iowa State University for a number of years. The seminar I offered each year provided me with a fresh and stimulating laboratory environment in which to explore new ideas and test their validity. My appreciation goes to the students who have participated in my seminar and shared their intellectual curiosity with me. This book has taken a number of years to complete, during which time my colleagues at Iowa State have given me support and encouragement. Special appreciation goes to Professors Don Hadwiger, Jorgen Rasmussen, and Donald Boles who did a critical reading of several chapters at the early stage. Special thanks also go to Betty Baird for proofreading the entire manuscript. My intellectual debt goes to many anonymous reviewers of *Public Administration Review* (PAR) and *Review of Public Personnel Administration* (ROPPA) who read my earlier papers and gave insightful comments and suggestions. Three chapters of this book rely on articles of mine that have appeared in PAR and ROPPA. I am grateful to these journals for granting me permission to use them in this book; the three articles are:

"Civil Liability of State and Local Governments," *Public Administration Review* 47 (March/April 1987): 160–170.

"Shaping Judicial Response to Gender Discrimination in Employment Compensation," *Public Administration Review* 49 (September/October 1989): 420–430.

"Affirmative Action and Judicial Standards of Review," *Review of Public Personnel Administration* 12 (Spring 1992).

Thanks are also due to Quorum Books of the Greenwood Publishing Group for their commitment to this project and their continued support of it. My final word of thanks is reserved for my wife, Dawn, and my son, Shawn—they persevered with me through this work.

# Public Personnel Administration and Constitutional Values

# 1

# A New Framework for Public Personnel Management: Toward Judicial Accountability

> The knowledge that a municipality will be liable for all of its injurious conduct, whether committed in good faith or not, should create an incentive for officials who may harbor doubts about the lawfulness of their intended actions to err on the side of protecting citizens' constitutional rights (Justice Brennan in *Owen v. City of Independence*).

The theory of public employment involves the relationship between a state, as employer, and its civil servants—who are otherwise ordinary citizens. This relationship involves the rights, expectations, and obligations between the two. Until the 1960s, U.S. courts assumed that government could restrict the First Amendment freedoms of public employees as it saw fit.[1] As the U.S. Supreme Court held in *Adler v. Board of Education* (1951), the petitioners (school teachers) "have the right under our law to assemble, speak, think and believe as they will . . . [but] they have no right to work for the State . . . on their own." It added, "They may work for the school system upon the reasonable terms laid down by the proper authorities. . . . If they do not choose to work on such terms, they are at liberty to retain their beliefs and associations and go elsewhere."[2] The Court also maintained that the Due Process Clause would not be applicable to public employees.[3]

During the last three decades, the Supreme Court, in a series of landmark decisions, has fundamentally altered this relationship by "constitutionalizing" it—that is, bringing the public employment relationship within the constitutional framework. Having done so, the judiciary has emerged as a senior partner in public management within the separation of powers framework.[4] What does this constitutionalization mean to today's public administrators? What different requirements, if any, does it place on them in the conduct of public personnel management? From the viewpoint of public administration research, one may also ask: What does this change suggest to the future of public personnel management theory? These are the questions I explore in this book.

By now, it is well known that the new employment relationship has fundamentally transformed the environment of public personnel management in the United States. It is also evident that the change requires a new framework for personnel management—a framework that is grounded in constitutional values. What is not entirely clear are the implications of this new requirement as it relates to public administration theory and the contours of its application. In this book, I will report that the new relationship is accompanied by a rapidly growing body of case law clarifying the uncertainties in application. I will also remind the readers that the management environment created by this case law is complex, full of uncertainty, yet inexorably demanding. Happily, a framework appears to be emerging that provides a new set of normative values grounded in the Constitution, including a multitude of case law principles. Taken together, the framework sets forth a new direction for research and a new requirement for public management. In this respect, I find that the differences between the classical employment relationship and the new one are profound, particularly in their underlying value premises. The differences, in fact, strike at the heart of American public administration theory.

*Pickering v. Board of Education* (1967) illustrates the point.[5] Marvin Pickering, a school teacher, disagreed with his school board's failed financial proposal and published a letter in a local newspaper criticizing the board policy. The school board fired him, based on disloyalty, disruption of workplace harmony, and harming the reputation of the school system. Under the classical public management model (as shown in *Adler*), the Supreme Court could have sustained the board decision because First Amendment freedoms would not apply to this teacher. Under the new model,[6] however, the Court required the board to carefully examine its need to restrict free speech of the school teachers against the constitutional right of these teachers, as citizens, to speak out on matters of public concern. Since the board had failed to do so, the Court ruled that the board action was unconstitutional.

The new framework makes demands on public administrators in many ways. It demands that administrators—superiors or subordinates—be fair, reasonable, and respectful of others' rights and privacy; it also demands that they be cognizant of the legal and constitutional implications of their possibly wrongful action. As the Supreme Court has held time and again in recent years, public administrators at all levels may be held personally liable for damages—compensatory and punitive—should their wrongful action result in the violation of other's rights.[7] It may be inconsequential, according to the Court, whether they actually knew or understood the rights in issue. As the Court wrote unequivocally, they can be held personally liable if their conduct violates "clearly established . . . constitutional rights of which a reasonable person would have known."[8] In sum, the new framework makes it imperative that public administrators improve their "constitutional competence," to use Professor Rosenbloom's words.[9] This is not an easy task, given that so little emphasis is placed on constitutional principles in the present public administration curriculum.[10] It requires an empirical investigation to determine how extensively and deeply today's public managers have adopted this new philosophy of management. There is no doubt, however, that those who do not understand the new management philosophy will be frustrated, confused, and even dangerous—dangerous in that they can be a legal liability to their employer.[11]

## THE NATURE OF THE PUBLIC EMPLOYMENT RELATIONSHIP IN THE UNITED STATES

The public employment relationship in the United States is fundamentally different, as one may expect, from that in the private sector.[12] This is because employers in the public sector are governmental bodies, and the U.S. Constitution forbids governmental bodies from encroaching upon certain individual rights.

Ideally, the Constitution would have enumerated the limits of governmental authority over public service employees vis-à-vis the rights and freedoms these employees may exercise while in public service. This, of course, is not the case. In most countries, these demarcations are drawn explicitly in the constitution or code of laws. The entire issue of the public employment relationship in the United States, however, has been left to the realm of the "unwritten constitution." From the point of view of the U.S. Constitution, it is not possible to identify what specific rights the Constitution has guaranteed public employees and what authority the state might have over these employees. In the final analysis, the parameters of this rights-expectations-obligations question in the United States are determined by the judiciary as it interprets the Constitution.

That the public employment relationship in the United States evolves via case law presents characteristics not commonly seen in other democracies. Unlike the application of the formal law (statutory law) to identifiable situations, the case law approach relies on the method of the common law, deciding case by case and building on what previous courts have decided. This means that the U.S. constitutional system is designed to work and make progress, for the most part, when the existing rules and interpretations are challenged in court. I use the phrase "for the most part" because in our separation of powers arrangement, the legislative body has primary responsibility to "make all laws which shall be necessary and proper for carrying into Execution all foregoing Powers . . . vested in the Constitution."

As mentioned earlier, the federal judiciary in the 1960s completely reversed its earlier position on the public employment relationship by placing it under the constitutional purview. The Court decisions during this period can be viewed as the judiciary's challenge to the rise of the administrative state.[13] As Professor Rosenbloom wrote, "Since the 1950s, several Supreme Court Justices and federal judges have noted the challenges that large-scale and ubiquitous public administration poses to the constitutional and political order." After World War II, the federal government and several states adopted the loyalty-security program, severely curtailing the rights of public employees, as well as individual citizens. The program sought to exclude from federal service people who were believed to be disloyal to the United States. Under the program, the government placed in the "suspect" category those who read the *New York Times*, participated in the peace movement, or read Marxist literature. As can be expected, this policy generated a large number of lawsuits challenging the constitutionality of the postwar loyalty-security program. These lawsuits provided the judiciary with an ample opportunity to critically reexamine the validity of some of the classical judicial doctrines (such as the doctrine of privilege) that were undergirding the power of the administrative state. In a sense, bad laws provide the opportunity to test the Constitution. The Sedition Act of 1798 and the Espionage Act of 1917 also provided the occasion to expand the scope of First Amendment freedoms.

Another characteristic of the case law approach to the public employment relationship is its cumulative effect of creating rights and benefits. The rights and benefits tend to expand but cannot be taken away arbitrarily (without due process). As Justice White wrote in *Cleveland Board of Education v. Loudermill* (1985), "The right to due process is conferred, not by legislative grace, but by constitutional guarantee."[14] The American administrative state in the present century has expanded the domain of public goods tremendously in the form of rights, benefits, and entitlements. Under the new public employment relationship, the administrative state can create new benefits and entitlements but can no longer take them away without constitutionally protected due process. The beneficiaries do not have to take the "bitter with the sweet," accepting the unreasonable conditions of the provider.[15] As the so-called "bitter with sweet" doctrine is no longer found constitutionally tenable, it is the engine of the Due Process Clause that helps to expand employee rights.

The American public employment relationship is as complex as case law itself. It is adaptive, full of uncertainty, and develops only when it is challenged. The way it has been evolving is, indeed, deeply American in design, although many have been less than willing to appreciate it. It is, in fact, a system of positive constitutional law. As Professor Ostrom wrote, "Persons in a constitutional republic must be able to initiate and sustain causes of action in the protection of their constitutional rights and in the imposition of limits upon governmental authorities."[16] One wonders: How has it been possible that this important constitutional heritage escaped the scholarship of American public administration for so long?

## A DRIFT IN AMERICAN SCHOLARSHIP

Literature abounds to show that, historically, the study of public administration in the United States began with the doctrine of efficiency as its disciplinary foundation. As Woodrow Wilson wrote in his well-known essay "The Study of Public Administration," "The field of administration is a field of business."[17] He saw the civil service reform of 1883 as a "moral preparation," in Professor Wallace Sayre's words,[18] for making public administration "businesslike."

Since Wilson, the study of public administration has taken many different directions, but the focus has remained remarkably the same: the pursuit of efficiency in the administrative state. However it is cut, one cannot deny the fact that public administration researchers have been basically recasting the same concern that Alexander Hamilton wrote of in Federalist No. 70, long before Wilson: "Energy in the Executive is a leading character in the definition of good government. . . . It will only remain to inquire, what are the ingredients which constitute this energy?"[19] A central premise in Hamilton's thesis in the *Federalist Papers* is the executive supremacy in public administration. As Professor John Rohr traces the intellectual history in his popular book, *To Run a Constitution* (1986), American scholarship basically proceeded with an assumption that the entire executive power of the national government was vested in the president.[20] Thus, if we substitute "efficiency" for "energy," Hamilton's concern was the same for all—the Wilsonians, the proponents of scientific management, the human relations advocates, the administrative behaviorists, and the political economists: how to increase efficiency or how to create an efficient government. To them, a good government was an efficient government.

What has emerged from this disciplinary orientation is the field of contemporary public personnel administration, single-mindedly focusing on a narrow track of the science of personnel management. The topics popular in personnel textbooks, therefore, have been efficiency principles, including position classification, job evaluation, performance appraisal, merit pay, and POSDCORB training (Planning, Organizing, Staffing, Directing, Coordinating, and Budgeting).[21] On reflection, the classical writers in American public administration have failed to pay attention in their scholarship to the centrality of constitutional values in the design of American public administration—freedoms, liberty, fairness, and due process.

Constitutional values are at the core of democratic administration. Yet, as Professor Ostrom argued, American scholarship in public administration has rejected the theory of democratic administration in favor of the bureaucratic theory of administration based on the philosophy of efficiency.[22] This rejection was a fundamental error in the study of American public administration. Professor Rohr, in tracing the constitutional origin of the administrative state, takes up this theme and argues that nowhere in the Constitution is it written that the executive power is vested exclusively in the president. Under the separation of powers arrangement, Congress is supposed to share much of the executive power, from appointments to foreign policy-making.[23]

How could public administration scholars be so wrong when designing the field of public administration? Woodrow Wilson, Frank Goodnow, and Louis Brownlow were all constitutional scholars. According to a thesis advanced by Professor Rohr, these scholars took their signal from Publius (This was the pseudonym James Madison used in his Federalist Papers) but then proceeded differently. "At the founding of the Republic," Rohr argues, "there was a solid consensus that the primary purpose of government is the protection of individual rights." But since Anti-Federalists were afraid that the establishment of the strong national government would be a threat to individual rights, Publius tried to ease their concerns by arguing that only a strong government could protect individual rights effectively. Classical writers, including Professor Brownlow, joined Publius, according to Professor Rohr, in defending powerful government as instrumental for higher ends. For them, the higher ends were the realization of democracy, so they substituted "democracy" for individual rights—a serious departure from Publius.[24] It is no surprise that the Brownlow Report—one of the best pieces on the application of classical public administration theory—focused on the doctrine of efficiency while providing no serious discussion of the protection of individual rights as government's primary purpose.

The "politics of administration" school was somewhat an exception to this efficiency orientation, in that its goal was to liberate public administration from the Wilsonian system of efficiency and to redirect its inquiry toward the nexus between administration and democratic values.[25] While the proponents of politics of administration made their case strongly, the thrust of their inquiry was largely directed to the questions of politics, legitimacy, and political accountability. They were successful in reinstating the democratic administration, which Wilson and his contemporaries rejected. From the viewpoint of the public employment relationship, however, the politics of administration school did not go far enough to inquire into the nexus between public administration and the Constitution, particularly as it pertains to individual rights.

The judiciary, too, seemed to show little interest in the constitutional issues of public personnel administration, claiming no jurisdiction over the issues that, under the common law, belonged to the appointing authority. Even in the sphere of individual rights in general, the judiciary had not gone very far until the last half century.[26]

## EMERGING ETHOS IN THE NEW PERSONNEL MANAGEMENT

As discussed, much has changed during the last three decades, thanks to judicial intervention. As Professor David Rosenbloom observed in his seminal essay published in 1975, "the courts have almost completely transformed the nature of the constitutional position of public employees in the United States."[27] From the viewpoint of public administration theory, the change is nothing less than a rejuvenation of what Professor Ostrom called "the rejected alternative"—the democratic administration grounded in the theory of a positive Constitution.[28]

The new approach recognizes that American public administration operates within the constitutional framework of separation of powers, that the executive ought to be energetic but is not the sole source of executive power, that public administrators are not exclusively under the executive branch but are an embodiment of all three branches—executive, legislative, and judicial. In this approach, the courts play a senior partner's role in public management, demanding that administrators be accountable to the Constitution. The approach engenders a new administrative culture in which, as Professor Rohr envisioned, "[Public administrators] should learn to think like judges, as well as like legislators, and executives, because they are all three of these."[29]

The new approach does not negate the concept of efficiency as a concern of central importance. The courts have emphasized time and again that First Amendment freedoms are not absolute and that under certain circumstances, they may be compromised for the efficient functioning of a democratic system—without which First Amendment rights become a mockery.[30] In *Pickering*, for instance, the Court took pains to explain that the need of government to operate efficiently can be a compelling government interest sufficient to legitimize government regulation of employees' free speech. The Court made it clear that, although public employees do not lose their rights conferred by the Constitution because they have chosen to work for government, First Amendment rights should be balanced against the need of the state to operate efficiently.[31] In sum, the Court recognizes that efficiency is still essential for public administration. What it requires is that the administrative state pursue the goal of efficiency in a manner that is consistent with constitutional values.

During the past three decades, the courts have reviewed a number of cases dealing with public employee rights—the rights arising from the Constitution and laws. It is possible to identify a few broad principles that the Supreme Court has set forth for public management. These principles serve as a point of departure for public management and research as American public administration takes its journey beyond the bicentennial.

### Constitutionally Guaranteed Rights

The Constitution confers upon individual citizens certain fundamental rights (such as certain freedoms, due process, and equal protection) that government must respect. A long-standing doctrine in American public administration has been that these rights do not apply to public employees. The Constitution does not explicitly address this question, as it says little about public administration. In their wisdom, therefore, the judiciary has been relying on the old English common law, assuming that public office is a function of public law. If it were a function of public law, the tenure of office should be subject to public law and the appointing authority, and not subject to the Constitution. In his seminal article published in 1955, "The Emerging Doctrine of Privilege in Public Employment," Professor Arch Dotson called this theory the "doctrine of privilege." Under this doctrine, public employees are presumed to serve at the pleasure of the appointing authority. Therefore, as Dotson argued, "the government may impose upon the public employee any requirement it sees fit as conditional to employment."[32] Accordingly, constitutional protections would not apply equally to public employees as they do to individual citizens.

The history of public personnel administration in the United States attests to the fact that this doctrine indeed served as a basic framework for public law and management until the 1960s. During the 1960s and 1970s, the Supreme Court, in a series of cases—*Wieman v. Updegraff* (1952), *Slochower v. Board of Education* (1955), *Cramp v. Board of Public Instruction* (1961), *Sweezy v. New Hampshire* (1956), *Baggett v. Bullit* (1963), *Shelton v. Tucker* (1960), *Speiser v. Randall* (1957)—had rejected the privilege doctrine as "wooden" and "meaningless."[33] In 1967, in *Keyishian v. Board of Regents*, the Court once again rejected the privilege doctrine, this time in the context of academic freedom: "Our Nation is deeply committed to safeguarding academic freedom, which is of transcendent value to all of us and not merely to the teachers concerned. That freedom is, therefore, a special concern of the First Amendment, which does not tolerate laws that cast a pall of orthodoxy over the classroom."[34]

### Employment as a Property Right

The constitutionality of the privilege doctrine also has been challenged on the basis of the Due Process Clause. In 1972, in *Roth v. Board of Education*, the Court pronounced that it was abandoning the privilege doctrine once and for all, declaring that the expectation of continued employment creates a property interest that the Constitution protects. Once a property interest has been established, public employers may not take it away without constitutionally guaranteed due process. Somewhat problematic in this approach is what precisely would give rise to the expectation of continued employment. At one point, the Court believed that public policy, formal or de facto practice, would engender the expectation of continued employment.[35] At another time, however, the Court placed emphasis more on the language of the statute and how the courts interpret it than on customary practices.[36]

### Equal Protection and Discrimination

Another major development in public personnel administration in recent years involves the application of the equal protection guarantees of the Fourteenth Amendment. While the Equal Protection Clause literally guarantees everyone "equal protection of the laws" or simply "no discrimination," the phrase had been interpreted historically to mean "separate but equal," particularly as it relates to race (*Plessy v. Ferguson* [1896]). The separate but equal doctrine permitted employers, public or private, to legally engage in discriminatory practices in employment, education, housing, public transportation, public accommodations, and many other spheres of American life.

In 1954, in *Brown v. Board of Education*, the Court struck down the separate but equal doctrine, declaring that "in the field of public education the doctrine of 'separate but equal' has no place," and that segregation in public education is "a denial of the equal protection of the laws." The *Brown* decision galvanized the civil rights movement into a nationwide force.[37] In response, Congress passed the Civil Rights Act of 1964—almost 100 years after the ratification of the Fourteenth Amendment—to articulate (and expand) the meaning of the Equal Protection Clause. In this legislation, Congress made discrimination unlawful in education (Title VI) and employment (Title VII), among others, if it were based on race, color, religion, nationality, or sex. In 1972, Congress amended Title VII (Equal Employment Opportunity) to apply it to the public sector at all three levels—federal, state, and local.

As Title VII applies to personnel management, public policy is focused not only on the questions of damages (back pay, make-whole, and injunctive relief), but also on affirmative action or proactive measures. Here, technical challenges are found to be enormously complicated. For example, how may discrimination be objectively measured, and what different thresholds may the judiciary use for determining various damages? The law in this area is in great flux as the Court has been sharply divided over the issues. This means that public administrators must keep abreast of the rapidly developing case law in this area.

### Affirmative Action and the Constitution

Affirmative action is equally complicated, if not more so. Presently, it seems as though the Court has reached an impasse on the question of affirmative action even in a restricted sense. While some justices (Chief Justice Rehnquist and Justice Scalia in particular) insist that the Equal Protection Clause means that the Constitution is color-blind, permitting no racial or gender-based classifications whatsoever, others (Justices Powell, Brennan, and Marshall—all retired—and Justice Stevens) maintain that the Constitution allows remedial affirmative action, permitting the opportunity to correct the effects of past wrongs. To deal with this dilemma the Court has developed a complicated analytical framework for reviewing affirmative action complaints, but it often finds consensus difficult to achieve. In *University of California Regents v. Bakke* (1978),[38] the Court, in a plurality opinion, established that a carefully designed affirmative action program would not be constitutionally impermissible. Yet, a decade after *Bakke*, the Court still finds it difficult to achieve consensus over what such a carefully designed program should be. Again, public administrators are expected to follow closely the development of case law.

## Immunities and Liability of Governmental Bodies

Public service has its own hazards—suing and being sued for damages. Can the government, as the sovereign, be sued for damages when its supposedly collective action results in the violation of constitutionally and statutorily guaranteed individual rights? Can a public official be held personally liable for his or her own misconduct that results in the violation of other's rights? The written Constitution is silent on these subjects.

Since the Constitution says little about matters of governmental liability, the courts initially relied on the old English common law, which states that the king can not be sued in his own court. In practice, this conventional wisdom has been interpreted to mean that the sovereign must consent to be sued and, unless it has consented, it is absolutely immune from civil liability. The old English Crown did, in some cases, consent to accept civil complaints against the Crown.

The question is whether governments in the United States—federal, state, and local—have consented via legislation to be sued for damages. In 1947, Congress enacted the Federal Tort Claims Act, allowing civil damages against governmental officials in their personal capacity and limited claims against the United States.[39] Most state governments have followed by enacting restricted tort laws permitting civil damage suits against them.[40] With respect to local government liability, according to the Court in *Monell v. Department of Social Services of the City of New York* (1978),[41] Congress removed all immunities from local government entities when it enacted the Civil Rights Act of 1871.

The Fourteenth Amendment was ratified in 1867. As a way to enforce its provisions, Congress enacted the Civil Rights Act, declaring that state and local officials ("every person who, under color of any statute . . . of any State . . .) shall be liable for civil damages when their actions cause or contribute to the deprivation of individual rights, privileges, or immunities secured by the Constitution and laws. There had been a controversy in the

Supreme Court concerning whether the 1871 law (now codified as 42 U.S.C. Section 1983) included municipalities in the phrase "every person." Until 1978, the Court did not think that Section 1983 could be read to be the consent by municipalities for civil liability. In 1978, in *Monell v. Department of Social Services of the City of New York*, the Court reversed its earlier holding in *Monroe v. Pape* (1961),[42] declaring that Section 1983 did, indeed, remove the municipality's absolute immunity from liability for constitutional and statutory torts. As can be expected, the *Monell* decision changed the nature of the legal environment for public administration in general and particularly at the local level.

In 1989, in *Will v. Michigan Department of State Office*,[43] the Court gave another interpretation of the 1871 law exempting the states from Section 1983 liability. The Court believed that Section 1983 did not override the Eleventh Amendment establishing state jurisdiction over certain judicial matters. This meant that civil liability involving state governments (not officials) would be matters of state law.

### Personal Liability of Public Administrators

With regard to official liability (in the personal capacity), case law has been growing rapidly in recent years. While federal officials are subject to suit for constitutional and statutory torts, the Supreme Court has ruled time and again that state and local governmental officials are subject to Section 1983 liability. In 1991, in *Hafer v. Melo*,[44] the Court confirmed once again that state officials are included in the phrase "every person" of the 1871 statute so they may be held liable to civil damages, including compensatory and punitive damages, should their wrongful action violate the rights and privileges secured by the Constitution and federal laws.

If modern governments in the United States are called the "administrative state"—apparently because of their bureaucratic omnipresence—the recent Court decisions clearly challenge the administrative state by demanding that it be accountable to the judiciary. Recently, courts have been shaping an administrative environment in which governments and officials "may harbor doubts about the lawfulness of their intended actions to err on the side of protecting citizens' constitutional rights."[45]

These are among the new ethos that have emerged in contemporary American public administration. In the chapters that follow, we will witness a rich body of case law that touches upon virtually every aspect of administrative behavior. The chapters will make it clear that today's public administrators, or for that matter, public employees in general, may not be able to escape from judicial scrutiny in their conduct of public administration. On a positive side, they will find that a commitment to constitutional values enriches their administrative milieu, strengthens their moral and ethical convictions, and heightens the place of administration in a constitutional democracy.

## NOTES

1. Arch Dotson, "The Emerging Doctrine of Privilege in Public Employment," *Public Administration Review* 15 (Spring 1955), 77–88.

2. *Adler v. Board of Education*, 342 U.S. 485, 492 (1951).

3. *Bailey v. Richardson*, 341 U.S. 918 (1951).

4. David H. Rosenbloom, "Public Administrators and the Judiciary: The 'New Partnership,' " *Public Administration Review* 47 (January/February 1987), 75–83.

5. *Pickering v. Board of Education*, 391 U.S. 563 (1968).

6. This case represents a landmark decision on this subject, contributing to the development of a new framework for management that I explore in this study.

7. *Wood v. Strickland*, 420 U.S. 308 (1975); *Harlow v. Fitzerald*, 457 U.S. 800 (1982); *Will v. Michigan Department of State Police*, 109 S. Ct. 2304 (1989); *Hafer v. Melo*, 60 LW 4001 (November 5, 1991).

8. *Harlow v. Fitzerald*, 457 U.S. 800 (1982).

9. David H. Rosenbloom and James D. Carroll, *Toward Constitutional Competence: A Casebook for Public Administrators* (Englewood Cliffs, N.J.: Prentice Hall, 1990).

10. Rosemary O'Leary, "Response to John Rohr," *Public Administration Review* 49 (March/April 1989), 115.

11. Yong S. Lee, "Civil Liability of State and Local Government," *Public Administration Review* 47 (March/April 1987), 160–170.

12. Some may disagree with this point, arguing that public employees should not be treated any differently from private sector employees.

13. Rosenbloom, "Public Administrators," 76.

14. *Cleveland Board of Education v. Loudermill*, 105 S. Ct. 1487, 1493 (1985).

15. *Arnett v. Kennedy*, 416 U.S. 134 (1973).

16. Vincent Ostrom, *The Intellectual Crisis in American Public Administration* (University, Alabama: The University of Alabama Press, 1973), 104.

17. Woodrow Wilson, "The Study of Administration," *Political Science Quarterly* 2 (June 1887), 198–222.

18. Wallace Sayre, "The Triumph of Techniques over Purpose," *Public Administration Review* 8 (Spring 1948), 134–137. This is a book review essay on Paul Pigors and Charles A. Meyers, *Personnel Administration: A Point of View and a Method* (New York: McGraw Hill Books, 1947).

19. Alexander Hamilton, James Madison, John Jay, *The Federalist Papers* (Washington, D.C.: Universal Classics Library, 1901), 49–58.

20. John A. Rohr, *To Run a Constitution: The Legitimacy of the Administrative State* (Lawrence, Kan., University of Kansas Press, 1986).

21. Luther Gulick and L. Urwick, eds., *Papers on the Science of Administration* (New York: Institute of Public Administration, Columbia University, 1937).

22. Ostrom, *The Intellectual Crisis.*

23. Rohr, *To Run a Constitution*, 15–27.

24. Ibid., 147.

25. Marshall E. Dimock and Gladys O. Dimock, *Public Administration*, 3rd ed., (New York: Holt, Rinehart, and Winston, 1964). See in particular, chapter 8, "The Politics of Administration."

26. Anthony Lewis, *Make No Law* (New York: Random House, 1991), 67.

27. David H. Rosenbloom, "Public Personnel Administration and the Constitution: An Emergent Approach," *Public Administration Review* 35 (January/February 1975), 52.

28. Ostrom, *The Intellectual Crisis*, 102–105.

29. Rohr, *To Run a Constitution*, 185.

30. *United Public Workers of America v. Mitchell*, 330 U.S. 75 (1947).

31. The judicial concern for efficiency finds its root in nineteenth century "spoils politics." The Civil Service Act of 1883 was a challenge to the spoils system, and Congress rejected its premise as a design principle for public administration.

32. Dotson, "The Emerging Doctrine of Privilege."

33. See *Wieman v. Updegraff*, 344 U.S. 183 (1952); *Slochower v. Board of Education*, 350 U.S. 551 (1955); *Cramp v. Board of Public Instruction* 368 U.S. 278 (1961); *Sweezy v. New Hampshire*, 354 U.S. 234 (1956); *Baggett v. Bullit* 377 U.S. 360 (1963); *Shelton v. Tucker*, 364 U.S. 479 (1963).

34. *Keyishian v. Board of Regents*, 385 U.S. 589, 603 (1966).

35. *Perry v. Sinderman*, 408 U.S. 593 (1972).

36. *Bishop v. Wood*, 426 U.S. 341 (1976).

37. Lewis, *Make No Law*, see especially chapter 3, "Separate and Equal," pp. 15–33.

38. 438 U.S. 265 (1978).

39. Charles Wise, "Suits Against Federal Employees for Constitutional Violations: A Search for Reasonableness," *Public Administration Review* 45 (November/December 1985), 845–856.

40. W. Bartley Hildreth and Gerald J. Miller, "State and Local Officials and Their Personal Liability," in Jack Rabin and Don Dodd, eds., *State and Local Government Administration* (New York: Marcel Dekker, 1985), 245–264.

41. 436 U.S. 658 (1978).

42. 365 U.S. 167 (1961).

43. 109 S. Ct., 2304 (1989).

44. 60 LW 4001 (November 5, 1991).

45. *Owen v. City of Independence, Missouri*, 445 U.S. 622, 651 (1980).

# 2

---

# *Property Rights, Liberty, and Due Process Protection*

At the core of modern personnel management—whether in the public sector or the private sector—is a contractual relationship between the employer and the employee. The contract, formal or informal, defines the rights, obligations, and mutual expectations often evoked between the employer and the employee in adversarial situations.[1] The term "adversarial situation" may sound like a worst-case scenario, but it defines the bottom line in the design of personnel administration.

The concept of public employment as it has evolved in contemporary American constitutional law is unique and distinguished from that of private employment. While private sector employees are the so-called "at-will" employees—that is, they hold their job tenure at the pleasure of their employers—public sector employees cannot be said to work at the pleasure of their government employers. Of course, private sector employees receive a host of statutory protections, just as public sector employees do, with respect to child labor, collective bargaining, occupational safety and health, and workplace discrimination, just to name a few. Yet, public employees are guaranteed constitutional protection not afforded private employees because public employers are governmental bodies and the Constitution (the Fifth and Fourteenth Amendments) limits the power of government to take arbitrary action against individuals without due process of law. The Fourteenth Amendment of the Constitution declares: "No State shall . . . deprive any person of life, liberty, or property, without due process of law."

This is not what it used to be. The change is very recent. This chapter examines the evolution of the public sector employment relationship—the rights, expectations, and obligations between government employers and public service employees. In particular, it explores what type of employment the Constitution may protect, and what limitations it places on governmental bodies as employers. But first, a brief excursion is in order to put the development in a historical perspective.

## AT-WILL EMPLOYMENT AND THE CONSTITUTION

Public personnel administration in the United States is governed by a plethora of legislation, executive orders, and civil service regulations—including the Pendleton Act of 1883, the Lloyd-La Follette Act of 1914, the Personnel Classification Act of 1923, the Hatch Act of 1939, the Occupational Safety and Health Act of 1974, various Executive Orders, and the Civil Service Reform Act of 1978. Yet, until recently, the fundamental employment relationship was governed by the common law doctrine of privilege, meaning that public employees were at-will employees who worked at the pleasure of their employers and were subject only to statutory and civil service regulations. Under this doctrine, public employment was regarded as a privilege, not a right, and public employers were free to impose any conditions they saw fit upon public employment, within statutory limitations.[2] Political assessments (kickbacks) under the spoils system, patronage appointment, partisan requirements, loyalty oaths, and harsh restrictions on free speech and organizational membership were all conditions for public employment at one time or another, justified by the so-called privilege doctrine.

The application of the doctrine of privilege was dramatically illustrated during the early 1950s when the nation was engulfed with the "red scare" campaign. Dorothy Bailey, an employee of the Federal Security Agency, was terminated on the ground that she was disloyal to the United States. The loyalty investigation, conducted under Executive Order 9835, allegedly revealed that she was once a member of the Communist party and other organizations with communist affiliation. Miss Bailey testified before the Regional Loyalty Board of the Civil Service Commission—categorically denying all charges—and presented numerous witnesses and affidavits on her behalf. They were of no use. The board terminated her employment, concluding that "reasonable grounds exist for belief" that Bailey was disloyal to the United States. During the interrogation by the Loyalty Board, Bailey charged later, she was given no opportunity to examine the evidence presented against her, to confront her accusers, or even to know who her accusers were. She appealed to the Loyalty Review Board for review, but without success. She then brought suit in the U.S. Court of Appeals for the D. C. Circuit, complaining *inter alia* that she was deprived of her constitutionally protected due process rights. The D. C. Circuit responded that the Due Process Clause of the Fifth Amendment did not apply to government employees because "[g]overnment employment is not property nor a contract." Leading the panel, Judge Prettyman wrote:

> In absence of statute or ancient custom to the contrary, executive offices are held at the will of the appointing authority, not for life or for fixed terms. If removal be at will, of what purpose would process be? To hold office at the will of a superior and to be removable there from only by constitutional due process of law is not applicable unless one is being deprived of something to which he has a right.[3]

## PROPERTY RIGHTS AND DUE PROCESS PROTECTION

By the mid 1960s, however, the U.S. Supreme Court was on its way to discarding the doctrine of privilege. In *Keyishian v. Board of Regents* (1967),[4] which involved the First Amendment freedom of speech, the Court attacked the privilege doctrine, arguing that "public employment may [not] be conditioned upon the surrender of constitutional rights which could not be abridged by direct government action." In 1972, in *Board of Regents v. Roth*,[5] the Court looked at the doctrine of privilege in the context of the Fourteenth Amendment and rejected its use once and for all.

In *Roth*, the Court announced that public employment creates a property interest when it engenders the expectation of continued employment. What creates this expectation? Not the Constitution, said the Court, but statutes, rules, or understandings that secure certain benefits and entitlement to those benefits. To have a property interest in a benefit, therefore, a person must have "more than an abstract need or desire for it," certainly "more than a unilateral expectation of it"; he must have a contractual relationship—formal or implied—that fosters the expectancy of continued employment.

For classified (permanent) employees, this contractual relationship is generally defined by legal documents, including statutes, civil service regulations, and agency personnel policies. But for many other situations, the contractual relationship is not formally stipulated in writing but may be understood by inference or extrapolation from custom, usage, and mutual understandings. The absence of a formal contractual relationship presents many difficulties for its determination. Granted that the employee's expectation is central to the existence of a property interest, how would this expectation be determined for the purpose of a property interest? What might be the threshold for passing constitutional muster?

In *Board of Regents v. Roth*, David Roth was a nontenured assistant professor of political science at Wisconsin State University in Oshkosh with a contract for one academic year. Under Wisconsin law, nontenured faculty could acquire tenure as permanent employees only after four years of year-to-year employment. The rules promulgated by the Board of Regents stated in part, "During the time a faculty member is on probation, no reason for non-retention need be given." Prior to February 1, 1969, the university informed Mr. Roth that he would not be rehired for the following academic year, but did not give a reason for the decision, nor an opportunity to challenge it. Mr. Roth filed a lawsuit in the U.S. District Court for the Northern District of Wisconsin, complaining that the university failed to advise him of the reason for its decision, in violation of the Due Process Clause of the Fourteenth Amendment. The district court held for Mr. Roth, stating that the Fourteenth Amendment required the university to give a hearing to any teacher whose contract was not to be renewed, and to give reasons for its action. The court of appeals affirmed the district court holding. But the Supreme Court disagreed, observing that Mr. Roth's initial appointment warranted no property interest in employment and hence he had no claim of entitlement to reemployment. The Court observed:

> [T]he terms of the respondent's appointment secured absolutely no interest in re-employment for the next year. They supported absolutely no possible claim of entitlement to re-employment. Nor, significantly, was there any state statute or University rule or policy that secured his interest in re-employment or that created any legitimate claim to it. In these circumstances, the respondent surely had an abstract concern in being rehired, but he did not have a *property* interest sufficient to require the University authorities to give him a hearing when they declined to renew his contract of employment.[6]

It may be noted that in *Roth* the Court mainly focused on the formal written policy in connection with the expectation of continued employment. It did not delve into the nature of expectation that might possibly arise from the organization's de facto policy, custom, or usage. This was dealt with in *Perry v. Sindermann,*[7] a companion case to *Roth* addressed the same day. Robert Sindermann was an instructor in the Texas state college system from 1959 to 1969 under a series of one-year contracts. The state college system provided no formal tenure for its teachers. In May 1969, the Board of Regents voted not to offer Sindermann a new contract but did not provide official reasons for nonrenewal, although the unstated reason was his public criticism of the college administration. Sindermann took the Board of Regents to court, complaining that its failure to provide a hearing deprived him of his Fourteenth Amendment right to procedural due process. Initially, the district court held for the Regents, maintaining that Sindermann had no property interest in his job because the state college system in Texas had not instituted a formal tenure system. The court of appeals, however, disagreed, arguing that while the system had no formal tenure system, the employment practice in operation sufficiently created an expectancy of reemployment, hence, a property interest, which the Constitution protects. On certiorari, the Supreme Court agreed with the appeals court holding. The Court observed that although the Texas state college system instituted no formal tenure system, the guidelines of the Coordinating Board of Texas College and the University System created a de facto tenure program engendering the expectancy of a continued employment. The college's official faculty guide contained this statement about teacher tenure: "Odessa College has no tenure system. . . . The Administration of the College wishes the faculty member to feel that he has permanent tenure as long as his teaching services are satisfactory and as long as he displays a cooperative attitude toward his co-workers and his superiors, and as long as he is happy in his work." Having studied this statement the Court had this to say:

> A written contract with an explicit tenure provision clearly is evidence of a formal understanding that supports a teacher's claim of entitlement to continued employment unless sufficient "cause" is shown. Yet absence of such an explicit contractual provision may not always foreclose the possibility that a teacher has a "property" interest in re-employment. . . . A teacher, like the respondent, who has held his position for a number of years, might be able to show from the circumstances of this service—and from other relevant facts—that he has a legitimate claim of entitlement to job tenure. . . . There may be an unwritten "common law" in a particular university, like Odessa Junior College, that has no explicit tenure system even for senior members of its faculty, but that nonetheless may have created such a system in practice.[8]

The above passage makes it clear that when attention is focused on a common law practice, a great number of factors other than formal writing become relevant to personnel decision making. This is particularly true for probationary or indefinite temporary employees. Organizational culture, employment manuals, interpersonal communication, memorandums of understanding, and past practice are all factors that may be relevant to the equation. Analysis of continued expectation, indeed, can become complex, and the answer may not always be clear or predictable.

*Bishop v. Wood* (1976)[9] exemplifies such complexity. The case involved a city ordinance of Marion, North Carolina that was arguably vague regarding discharging city employees. The ordinance stipulated that a permanent employee may be discharged only if he fails to perform work up to the standards of his classification, or if he is negligent, inefficient, or unfit to perform his duties. Mr. Bishop, a police officer, was discharged without a hearing on the ground that he failed to follow orders, showed poor attendance at training sessions, and exhibited low morale and conduct unsuited an officer. Bishop filed a complaint in the U.S. District Court, contending that since the city ordinance classified him as a permanent employee, he had a property interest in his job and, therefore, was entitled to a pretermination hearing. The district court held, on the basis of its own understanding of state law, that Bishop was an at-will employee, working at the pleasure of the city. The court of appeals affirmed the district court holding. On certiorari, the Supreme Court, in a five to four majority, also upheld the lower court decision. Justice Stevens, delivering the opinion of the Court, reasoned that while "the city ordinance on its face may be read as conferring a property interest, it may also be construed as granting no right to continued employment, but merely conditioning an employee removal on compliance with certain specified procedures."[10] Unable to resolve the ambiguity of Marion's city ordinance, the majority decided to side with the lower court interpretation of state law borrowed from the North Carolina Supreme Court in *Still v. Lance* in 1971.[11]

Four Justices (Brennan, White, Blackmun, and Marshall) dissented, arguing that the decision was an error in light of *Board of Regents v. Roth*. Justice Brennan, invoking the *Roth* dictrum that "property interests . . . can arise from existing rules or understandings that derive from an independent source such as state law," challenged that the majority reasoning was out of line. Instead of relying on a lower court interpretation of state law, the Court should have inquired "whether it was objectively reasonable for the employee to believe he could rely on continued employment." That would require at a minimum "an analysis of the common practices utilized and the expectations generated by [the city] and the manner in which the local ordinances would reasonably be read by [the city] employees."[12]

In light of *Bishop*, one may surmise that the determination of a property interest in public employment is still not without problems. While the objective expectation of continued employment is central to an analysis of whether a property interest exists, the mutual expectation—between the employer and the employee—is equally critical in such analysis. In *Bishop*, the majority gave greater weight to state law and the way in which state law was interpreted by state courts because the property interest in that case was a state issue. As the Court maintained, "the federal court is not an appropriate forum in which to review the multitude of personnel decisions that are made daily by public agencies," even though mistakes would inevitably be made in the process.[13] Some interpret this as a sign that the Court wishes to "deconstitutionalize" public personnel issues. Whether such an attempt is deliberate or not, the logic of *Bishop* is not significantly at variance with the theory of property rights as defined in *Roth*—insofar as the relationship between expectation and a property right is concerned. What is unclear, however, is why the Court accepted the lower court understanding of state law at its face value rather than providing a guideline for determining the expectancy of continued employment.

## LIBERTY AND DUE PROCESS PROTECTION

As in property rights, the central question in the analysis of liberty is what it means in connection with public employment and what employer action may be considered an intrusion into individual liberty that the Constitution protects. In *Board of Regents v. Roth*, the Court emphasized that "[l]iberty and property are broad and majestic terms . . . purposefully left to gather meaning from experience."[14] In this vein, the Court construed liberty to denote "not merely freedom from bodily restraint but also the right of the individual to contract, to engage in any of the common occupations of life, to acquire useful knowledge, to marry, establish a home and bring up children, to worship God according to the dictates of his own conscience, and to generally enjoy those privileges long recognized . . . as essential to the orderly pursuit of happiness by free men."[15] In the 1970s the Court was well on its way to expanding the scope of liberty in the public employment context.

In *Roth v. Board of Regents*, the Court recognized that a false charge damaging one's standing in his community would be an issue of liberty actionable under the Due Process Clause. According to the majority, this was not the case for Mr. Roth, however. The university simply did not renew his contract, period. The Court, therefore, did not think that the university's decision not to renew Roth's contract had negative implications about his good name, reputation, or integrity. In *Bishop v. Wood*, the petitioner (Mr. Bishop) argued that his liberty—good name, reputation, honor, or integrity—was impaired by false explanation of his discharge. A narrow majority of the Court did not think that his liberty was impaired by false explanations because there was no public disclosure of the reasons for his discharge. A public disclosure was an issue in *Owen v. City of Independence* (1980).[16] While summarily discharging Mr. Owen as chief of police, the city council released to the press an allegedly false statement impugning his honesty and integrity. The Court held without difficulty that Mr. Owen had been deprived of his constitutionally protected liberty without due process.

At issue in *Cleveland Board of Education v. LaFleur* (1974)[17] was a policy requiring a mandatory leave of absence due to pregnancy. The policy set arbitrary dates for the commencement of leave. The Court held that the mandatory maternity leave policy with dates set arbitrarily was an unnecessary intrusion to one's liberty protected by the Constitution—to marry, establish a home, and bring up children. Grooming regulations for male police officers were an issue in *Kelley v. Johnson* (1976).[18] The Court observed that, although the "choice of personal appearance is an ingredient of an individual's personal liberty," such regulations would not be irrational, hence not unconstitutional, when demonstrably job-related. To persuade a court otherwise, the complainant must demonstrate that there is no rational connection between the regulation and public policy goals—in this case, the promotion of public safety via an espirit de corps contributed to by the grooming regulation.

As the Court recognized repeatedly, the meaning of liberty is broad and timeless. Thus, it can be expected that the breadth and scope of its application will continue to expand in connection with, but not limited to, public employment. It is essential that public administrators keep abreast of case law so they may promote constitutional values in public employment.

## PROCEDURAL DUE PROCESS

The Fourteenth Amendment declares in part, "No state shall . . . deprive any person of life, liberty, or property, without due process of law." In the context of public employment, this means that once the existence of a property interest or liberty in connection with one's employment has been established, the government as an employer may not take away these rights without due process of law. The question is what procedures are required in such adversarial decision making. At the federal level, the Lloyd-La Follette Act of 1912, now codified as 5 U.S.C. Section 7501, recognizes that classified civil service employees have a property interest in their employment, so they are entitled to a posttermination hearing (Subsection b). It may be noted that for all practical purposes, the posttermination hearing is an ex post facto ritual taking place sometime after the termination decision has already been made, with a chief aim being to legitimize the initial decision. *Arnett v. Kennedy* (1974)[19] illustrates the point. In this case, Wayne Kennedy, a nonprobationary federal employee in the Chicago regional office of the Office of Economic Opportunity was discharged on the ground that he accused his superiors of bribery without proof and in reckless disregard of facts known to him. In accordance with the Lloyd-La Follette Act and the civil service regulations supplementing the act, he was advised of his right to a formal hearing on appeal, but not a pretermination hearing. Instead of making an administrative appeal, Kennedy decided to file a complaint directly in the U.S. District Court for the Northern District of Illinois, contending that although the Lloyd-La Follette Act granted him a property interest, it failed to require a pretermination hearing in violation of the Due Process Clause of the Fifth Amendment. He insisted that the Due Process Clause entitled him to a pretermination hearing—before damage is done. The district court agreed with him, concluding that "the discharge procedures authorized by the Act and the attendant Civil Service regulations denied [Kennedy] due process because they failed to provide for a trial-type hearing before an impartial agency official prior to removal."[20]

On certiorari, the Supreme Court was unable to produce a majority opinion. The plurality, led by Justice Rehnquist, sidestepped the issue by admonishing the complainant, "It is an elementary rule of constitutional law that one may not retain the benefits of an Act while attacking the constitutionality of one of its important conditions."[21] In other words, since the Lloyd-La Follette Act granted a cause for Kennedy's legal action, he could not at the same time attack the constitutionality of the same act. Rehnquist observed that "where the grant of a substantive right is inextricably intertwined with the limitations on the procedures which are to be employed in determining that right, a litigant in the position of appellee must take the bitter with the sweet."[22] But other justices in dissent voiced an objection, urging the Court to construe the Due Process Clause as requiring that a hearing be held before a permanent employee is terminated for alleged misconduct.

The issue was revisited in 1985 in *Cleveland Board of Education v. Loudermill* and in *Parma Board of Education v. Donnelly*[23] reversing *Kennedy*. In these cases, James Loudermill and Richard Donnelly, in suits separately filed at the outset, challenged the constitutionality of the Ohio statute under which they were dismissed without a pretermination hearing. While Loudermill, a security guard, was fired because of his dishonesty in filling out the employment application, Donnelly, a bus mechanic, was fired because he had failed to take an eye examination. The District Court for the Northern District of Ohio dismissed the complaints under the so-called "bitter with sweet" approach: "Because the very statute that created the property right in continued employment also specified the procedures for discharge, and because those procedures were followed, Loudermill was, by definition, afforded all the process due."[24] The court of appeals disagreed, maintaining that "the compelling private interest in retaining employment, combined with the value of presenting evidence prior to dismissal, outweighed the added administrative burden of a pretermination hearing."[25] On certiorari, the Supreme Court attacked the "bitter with sweet" principle, arguing that the approach misconceived the constitutional guarantee. Leading the Court, Justice White emphasized that property interests are created not by the Constitution but by existing rules or understandings that stem from an independent source such as state law, and that, once conferred, their deprivation is subject to federal law. "The right to due process," declared the justice, "is conferred, not by legislative grace, but by constitutional guarantee."[26] The minimum procedural requirements, therefore, are "not diminished by the fact that the State may have specified its own procedures that it may deem adequate for determining the preconditions to adverse official action."

With respect to a pretermination hearing itself, the Court recognized that "the severity of depriving a person of the means of livelihood outweighs in significance the governmental interest in immediate termination." Moreover, dismissals for cause often involve factual disputes that may best be clarified by a pretermination hearing. Hence, the Court held that "affording the employee an opportunity to respond prior to termination would impose neither a significant administrative burden nor intolerable delays."[27] Having said that, the Court acknowledged that the pretermination hearing need not be elaborate; it can be "something less than a full evidentiary hearing." "[T]he formality and procedural requisites for the hearing can vary," instructed the Court, "depending upon the importance of the interests involved and the nature of the subsequent proceedings." What is absolutely necessary in the process are "notice and an opportunity to respond"—the opportunity to present reasons, either in person or in writing, why proposed action should not be taken.

## SUMMARY AND CONCLUSION

To many, especially those who are familiar with private sector personnel administration, it is difficult to understand why public employees should be treated any differently from private sector employees with respect to dismissal or taking disciplinary action. The answer is simple. It is because their employers are governmental entities, and the Constitution says government shall not deprive any individual of his or her life, liberty, or property arbitrarily—without due process of law. The Constitution, of course, does not create property rights any more than it creates life or liberty. But the framers of the Constitution agreed that life, liberty, and property should be protected by the constitutional requirement of due process.

At the heart of the inquiry in public employment is whether government confers a property interest when it hires an individual into a permanent (or classified) position. Until the early 1970s, the judiciary maintained that public employment was a privilege and that it did not confer a property interest or liberty. In a series of landmark decisions in the late 1960s and early 1970s, the U.S. Supreme Court reversed its previous position, recognizing that, under certain circumstances, public employment creates a property interest that the Constitution protects. Employment creates a property interest when it engenders the expectation of continued employment. The sources of this expectation are found in statutes, rules, and conventions. Although the statutes and conventions can create a property interest, they cannot take away the property without constitutionally guaranteed due process. The Court also held that in the employment context, due process requires both a pretermination hearing and a postter-mination hearing—although the former need not be elaborate.

An analytical question at this point is how one should interpret public law, agency regulations, and organizational practices that have implications as to the expectancy of continued employment. The Court has been reluctant to provide an analytical framework for such interpretation. Instead, it has relied on state law or the ways in which lower courts interpret public law. This is an issue yet to be addressed by the judiciary.

Some may contend that under the existing civil service regulations, it is difficult, if not impossible, to dismiss unproductive employees. It is argued that the constitutional due process protection affirmed by the Court completely ties the hands of public personnel managers. There is an element of truth in this argument; the due process of law can slow down personnel administration, forcing public managers to compromise the principle of efficiency. This is not a trivial issue. Yet, one should note that an equally—if not more—important value in public administration is that public employers "do it right," even if it is a little slow and costly. When government is allowed to deviate from what is right and fair, it creates a possibility of tyranny, which the framers of the Constitution rejected once and for all. In this sense, one should not dwell upon a view that the due process protection ties the hands of public managers, but rather find ways to improve efficiency within the constitutional framework.

## NOTES

1. Jay M. Shafritz, Albert C. Hyde, and David H. Rosenbloom, *Personnel Management in Government*, 3rd ed. (New York: Marcel Dekker, 1986), 230.

2. Arch Dotson, "The Emerging Doctrine of Privilege in Public Employment," *Public Administration Review* 15, no. 2, (Spring 1955), 77–88.

3. *Bailey v. Richardson*, 86 U.S. App. D.C. 248, 260 (1950).

4. *Keyishian v. Board of Regents*, 385 U.S. 589 (1967).

5. *Board of Regents v. Roth*, 408 U.S. 564 (1972).

6. Ibid., 578.

7. *Perrry v. Sindermann*, 408 U.S. 593 (1972).

8. Ibid., 691–692.

9. *Bishop v. Wood*, 426 U.S. 341 (1976).

10. Ibid., 345.

11. *Still v. Lance*, 279 N.C. 254 (1971).

12. *Bishop v. Wood*, 354 (Justice Brennan dissenting).

13. Ibid., 349.

14. *Board of Regents v. Roth*, 571.

15. Ibid., 572.

16. *Owen v. City of Independence*, 445 U.S. 621 (1980).

17. *Cleveland Board of Education v. LaFleur*, 414 U.S. 632 (1974).

18. *Kelley v. Johnson*, 425 U.S. 238 (1976).

19. *Arnett v. Kennedy*, 416 U.S. 134 (1974).

20. Ibid., 139.

21. Ibid., 153.

22. Ibid.

23. *Cleveland Board of Education v. Loudermill*, 470 U.S. 532 (1985); 105 S. Ct. 1487 (1985).

24. Ibid., 1490.

25. Ibid., 1491.

26. Ibid., 1493.

27. Ibid., 1495.

# 3

# *Free Speech and*
# *Organizational Politics*

Chapter 2 concluded that the right of a public employee to procedural due process is conditioned upon the showing of a property interest in employment or a deprivation of liberty related to the employment. In regard to the substantive rights guaranteed by the First Amendment, the language of the Constitution is direct and without qualification: "Congress shall make no law . . . abridging the freedom of speech, or of the press; the right of the people peaceably to assemble, and to petition the Government for a redress of grievances." At issue in public management is whether government, as an employer, must respect the First Amendment rights of its civil servants in the same way as it respects an ordinary citizen's rights, or if it may constitutionally treat the employee differently because he or she is working for that government. The answer to this question is complex and, indeed, goes to the heart of the history of American public administration. This chapter traces the development of case law principles shaping public employees' rights to free speech, and organizational politics relating to patronage practice, partisan political activity, and organizational activity in general.

## THE DOCTRINE OF PRIVILEGE

As discussed in chapter 2 in the context of the public employment relationship, the long-standing doctrine in American public administration was that individuals hired to work for government surrendered, as a price for employment, their constitutionally guaranteed rights. What followed, then, was a belief that government, as an employer, could legitimately place restrictions in any way it saw fit on the freedoms guaranteed by the Constitution. According to this doctrine, government, as an employer, should be able to discipline its employees if it were to function efficiently, and to that end, it could restrict their freedoms, when necessary. But the First Amendment expressly forbids government to arbitrarily interfere with the fundamental rights conferred upon individuals. Herein lies a dilemma: which principle governs public personnel management? The common law solution to this dilemma was to treat public employees as a special class generally exempt from constitutional scrutiny. Arch Dotson named this approach the "doctrine of privilege,"[1] referring to Judge Holmes' remark in *McAuliffe v. New Bedford*, 155 Mass. 216 (1892): "The petitioner may have a constitutional right to talk politics, but he has no constitutional right to be a policeman." This was the response that Judge Holmes gave to Mr. McAuliffe, a policeman in New Bedford, who complained that he was unconstitutionally dismissed from his job because of his membership in a political committee. Holmes explained that "There are few employments for hire in which the servant does not agree to suspend his constitutional rights of free speech . . . On the same principle the city may impose any reasonable condition upon holding offices within its control."[2]

Today, not many would agree with Judge Holmes's view. In fact, the judiciary has discarded it completely. But his view—the doctrine of at-will employment—characterized much of the history of American public administration. In this connection, patronage appointment and dismissal in the pre-civil service reform period may be viewed as a wholesale application of the privilege doctrine. Insisting that "to the victor belongs the spoils," the winners of an election during that period took it as their birthright to distribute government jobs to their party loyalists. Many believed that this was what democracy was all about—to carry out the will of the people, to nurture the growth of political parties, and to build American democracy.[3] No one challenged the practice on the First Amendment ground.

Patronage appointment and removal was as old as the republic, and it went hand in hand with the doctrine of privilege. When the practice was challenged, it was not on the ground of First Amendment rights but on the ground of efficiency. Consequently, the nineteenth century civil service reform did not deal with the doctrine of privilege at all. The reformers' concern was about the evils of the spoils politics: corruption and inefficiency.[4] At the end, the patronage practice brought President John Garfield to an assassin's bullet in the fateful summer of 1881; the assassin was a disappointed federal job seeker, a lawyer named Charles Guiteau.

Garfield's tragedy was the last straw signalling the unraveling of the spoils era. And in Herbert Agar's words, "The public at last was ready for civil service reform."[5] In 1883, congressional Democrats and Republicans—for political reasons—hastily forged bipartisan support for the Pendleton Act, the first merit-based civil service legislation in the United States. The congressional Republicans, who lost their narrow majority in the 1882 mid term election, had wished that the civil service reform bill would save the federal positions of their party loyalists. With the passage of the act, the nation embarked upon a new era of the public service based on competition, discipline, and political neutrality.

The nineteenth century reform marked the triumph of the state interest over individual rights. While the 1883 Reform Act guaranteed the political neutrality of the civil service, this guarantee had a "give-and-take." On the one hand, it attempted to protect the tenure of civil service employees from patronage dismissal; on the other hand, it restricted their freedom to get involved in the political process. This restriction then was extended to other First Amendment freedoms whenever deemed necessary.

As discussed in chapter 2, Dorothy Bailey complained that she was unconstitutionally dismissed because of her political beliefs, activities, or affiliations. The Court of Appeals for the D.C. Circuit, however, told her that although the First Amendment guaranteed free speech and assembly, it did not apply to civil servants.[6] *Adler v. Board of Education* in 1951 was another case that upheld the primacy of state interest over individual freedoms.[7] In *Adler*, New York public school teachers challenged the constitutionality of the education law known as the Feinberg Law. The Feinberg Law required the State Board of Regents to promulgate a list of organizations considered subversive and to provide rules under which membership in any organization so listed "shall constitute prima facie evidence of disqualification for employment in New York school systems." On certiorari, the Supreme Court upheld the law, pronouncing that school teachers must comply with reasonable free speech restrictions laid down by the proper authorities. And the Court declared, "If they do not choose to work on such terms, they are at liberty to retain their beliefs and associations and go elsewhere."[8] The Court, per Justice Minton, reasoned:

A teacher works in a sensitive area in a schoolroom. There he shapes the attitude of young minds towards the society in which they live. In this, the state has vital concern. It must preserve the integrity of the schools. That the school authorities have the right and the duty to screen the officials, teachers, and employees as to their fitness to maintain the integrity of the schools as a part of ordered society, cannot be doubted. One's associates, past and present, as well as one's conduct, may properly be considered in determining fitness and loyalty. From time immemorial, one's reputation has been determined in part by the company he keeps. In the employment of officials and teachers of the school system, the state may very properly inquire into the company they keep, and we know of no rule, constitutional or otherwise, that prevents the state, when determining the fitness and loyalty of such persons, from considering the organizations and persons with whom they associate.

If, under the procedure set up in the New York law, a person is found to be unfit and is disqualified from employment in the public school system because of membership in a listed organization, he is not thereby denied the right of free speech and assembly. His freedom of choice between membership in the organization and employment in the school system might be limited, but not his freedom of speech or assembly, except in the remote sense that limitation is inherent in every choice.[9]

## THE RESTORATION OF FIRST AMENDMENT FREEDOMS

Some fifteen years later, the *Adler* issue was revisited in *Keyishian v. Board of Regents*.[10] In *Keyishian*, several faculty members of the State University of New York challenged the loyalty oath required by the Feinberg Law. Section 3021 of the Feinberg Law required the disqualification of an employee involved with advising, teaching, advocating, or distributing the doctrine of forceful overthrow of government. Under the law, every teacher was required to sign a certificate that he or she was not a Communist. Teachers who were Communists were required to communicate it to the president of the university. The law required nonteaching staff to answer in writing under oath: "Have you ever advised or taught or were you ever a member of any society or group of persons which taught or advocated the doctrine that the Government of the United States or any political subdivision thereof should be overthrown or overturned by force, violence or any unlawful means?"

The *Keyishian* majority reversed the *Adler* decision, stating that even though the governmental purpose of protecting its education system from subversion is legitimate and substantial, government may not pursue that purpose by means that might stifle fundamental personal liberties. If it must restrict freedoms, the means selected must be narrowly tailored. The Court, per Justice Brennan, reasoned, "Our Nation is deeply committed to safeguarding academic freedom, which is of transcendent value to all of us and not merely to the teachers concerned. That freedom is therefore a special concern of the First Amendment, which does not tolerate laws that cast a pall of orthodoxy over the classroom."[11] And "because First Amendment freedoms need breathing space to survive, government may regulate in the area only with narrow specificity."[12]

The Court also agreed with the faculty at the State University of New York that the New York statute was unconstitutionally vague and overbroad. The Court challenged the statute, questioning at what point advising and teaching might become a seditious act of advocacy subject to criminal penalty. "Does the teacher who informs his class about the precept of Marxism or the Declaration of Independence violate this prohibition? . . . And does the prohibition of distribution of matter containing the doctrine bar histories of the evolution of Marxist doctrine or tracing the background of the French, American, or Russian Revolutions?" Uncertain of where a teacher should draw the line between seditious and nonseditious utterances and acts, he would try to "stay as far as possible from utterances or acts which might jeopardize his living by enmeshing him in this complicated [plan]." This uncertainty invites caution that stifles the "free play of the spirit which all teachers ought . . . to cultivate and practice."[13] The Court saw this as constitutionally unacceptable.

The Court also reasoned that disqualification for employment based on membership rests on the doctrine of "guilt by association," and it declared that such doctrine is repugnant to the spirit of the First Amendment.[14] The Court, once again, rejected the premise that public employees sacrifice their constitutionally guaranteed freedoms as a price for working for government.[15]

## STATE INTEREST V. INDIVIDUAL RIGHTS

What we saw in *Keyishian* was a major shift of a paradigm in public personnel administration in the application of the First Amendment—from the primacy of state interest to the centrality of individual rights. Likewise, *Board of Education v. Roth* (as discussed in chapter 2) discarded the doctrine of privilege in the context of the Fifth and Fourteenth Amendments, extending to public employees the protection of procedural due process. Taken together, *Keyishian* and *Roth*—there are also other related cases—have constitutionalized American public personnel administration, bringing it directly under the purview of the Constitution and subjecting it to constitutional scrutiny. Yet, *Keyishian* and *Roth* did not provide a comprehensive framework for new personnel policy. The details were to evolve via what one may call an "idiographic approach."[16] What soon emerged in this idiographic approach was the problem of balancing two competing interests: (1) the need of government, as an employer, to control and discipline its civil servants, and (2) the interest of civil servants, as citizens, to exercise the rights guaranteed by the Constitution. Analysis of post-*Keyishsian* cases provides several case law principles which form a body of law that juxtaposes and attempts to reconcile the two competing interests. The principles include:

1. Public employees assume "dual citizenships"—one as government employees and the other as ordinary citizens—and they have not surrendered their constitutional rights just because they have decided to work for government. See *Keyishian v. Board of Education*, 385 U.S. 589 (1967).

2. Government, as an employer, may not stifle the First Amendment rights of individuals who happen to be public employees. See *Keyishian v. Board of Education*.

3. The First Amendment rights are not absolute; rather, under some circumstances, they may be compromised (sacrificed) for the efficient functioning of a democratic system—without which First Amendment freedoms would become a mockery. See *United Public Workers of America v. Mitchell*, 330 U.S. 75 (1947).

4. Government may regulate First Amendment freedoms without violating the Constitution when it deems necessary. See *United Public Workers of America v. Mitchell*; *Elrod v. Burns*, 427 U.S. 347 (1976).

5. The interest of government must be shown to be a need of paramount (or overriding) importance. The need cannot be justified for the sake of convenience. The need must be specific, not overbroad; realistic, not abstract. See *Sugarman v. Dougall*, 413 U.S. 634 (1973); *Elrod v. Burns*.

6. Government, as an employer, may not regulate its employees' speech on matters of public concern—unless state interest is of overriding importance. State interests of overriding importance include, but are not limited to: (1) the need for discipline and workplace harmony, (2) the need for confidentiality, (3) the need for carrying out assigned duties, and (4) the need for personal loyalty and confidence. See *Pickering v. Board of Education*, 391 U.S. 563 (1968).

7. Government, as an employer, may constitutionally restrict an employee's free speech on matters of personal concern, including personal vendetta. See *Connick v. Meyers*, 461 U.S. 138 (1983).

8. Government, as an employer, may not interfere with an employee's freedom of association—unless it can demonstrate its interest is of vital importance. The state interests of vital importance in a democracy include, but are not limited to, national security and political (or electoral) accountability. See *Keyishian v. Board of Education*; *Elrod v. Burns*.

9. If and when First Amendment freedoms must be restricted, the means selected must be the least restrictive or narrowly tailored to serve the specific purpose. Restrictions that are vague or overbroad are constitutionally impermissible. See *Sugarman v. Dougall*; *Elrod v. Burns*.

These are fairly specific principles, although room still exists for interpretation as new circumstances arise. Since this balancing approach juxtaposes the state interest against individual rights, it can be expected that the Court pendulum may swing in either direction, depending on who sits on the bench and is able to forge the majority opinion. Some justices (for example, Burger, Rehnquist, Scalia, and O'Connor) clearly have been on the side of state interest—when the two were competing—while others (for example, Brennan, Marshall, Blackmun, Stevens, and White) have been on the side of individual rights. The sections below examine how these principles have been applied to free speech and partisan political activity.

## PUBLIC CRITICISMS AND OTHER EXPRESSIVE CONDUCTS

In 1968, in *Pickering v. Board of Education*,[17] the Court once again rejected the doctrine of privilege and reaffirmed the *Keyishian* principle that "teachers may not constitutionally be compelled to relinquish the First Amendment rights they would otherwise enjoy as citizens." Likewise, the Court proclaimed that teachers have the First Amendment protection "to comment on matters of public interest in connection with the operation of the public schools in which they work." Having said that, however, the Court acknowledged that the state, as an employer, would have an interest in regulating the speech of its employees if their free speech were to impede the efficiency of governmental operation. The question is how one may "arrive at a balance between the interests of the teacher, as a citizen, in commenting upon matters of public conern and the interest of the State, as an employer, in promoting the efficiency of the public services it performs through its employees."[18]

To the Court, the answer rested upon the analysis of the nature of the speech made by the public employee, on the one hand, and the importance of the state interest, on the other. With respect to the nature of speech, the Court's concern was whether the speech (e.g., criticism) falls in the public domain or in the private domain. Whereas private speech may not be constitutionally protected, the Court found it essential that speech addressing "matters of public concern" be constitutionally protected. "[F]ree and open debate," emphasized the Court, "is vital to informed decision-making by the electorate." According to the Court, the public concern doctrine also extended to criticisms made by public employees directed at their nominal superiors.[19] While exercising this freedom, however, the Court insisted that the speech be made in "good faith."[20] The Constitution does not protect false statements made "with knowledge of their falsity or in reckless disregard for their truth or falsity."[21]

Concerning the state interest, the Court identified several circumstances in which government may legitimately restrict an employee's freedom of speech—even though the speech touches on matters of public concern. David Rosenbloom paraphrased the circumstances succinctly:

1. The need for maintaining discipline and harmony in the workplace.
2. The need for confidentiality.
3. The possibility that an employee's position is such that his statements might be hard to counter due to his presumed greater access to factual information.
4. The situation in which an employee's statements impede the proper performance of duties.
5. The case where the statements are so without foundation that the individual's basic capability to perform his duties comes into question.
6. The jeopardizing of a close and personal loyalty and confidence.[22]

There may be other circumstances that warrant governmental restrictions on an employee's free speech. As we will discuss shortly, government may constitutionally prohibit public employees from delivering political speeches in partisan gatherings. At any rate, the task is to determine if governmental interests override the interest of a public employee as a private citizen. This means that government, as an employer, must carry the initial burden of demonstrating the presence of such vital interests, as well as how these interests have been specifically or materially impaired by its employee's speech—provided that the speech was made truthfully. The failure to demonstrate such interests would result in a finding that the government violated the public employee's First Amendment rights.

In *Pickering*, where a school teacher was dismissed for writing a letter in a local newspaper criticizing the school board's allocation of school funds, the Court scrutinized the interests of the school board and their importance vis-à-vis the interest of Mr. Pickering, as a school teacher and as a citizen, to speak in public on matters of public concern. As the record revealed, the board made allegations that Pickering's conduct (1) included false statements, (2) damaged the professional reputation of the board and the superintendent, (3) would be disruptive of faculty discipline, and (4) tended to foment controversy, conflict, and dissension among the board, teachers, administrators, and the residents of the district. The Court examined each of these charges at great length. Finding no material evidence that justified the charges, the Court determined that the board's dismissal of the plantiff failed to pass constitutional muster.

Concerning Mr. Pickering's statement on the management of the school funds, the Court believed that the issue was a matter of legitimate public concern. "It is essential that teachers as a special class, should be able to speak out freely on such questions without fear of retaliatory dismissal." With regard to the allegation of a false and erroneous statement on dollar expenditures, the Court suggested that the dollar figures were "matters of public record" and "[t]he Board could easily have rebutted [his] errors by publishing the accurate figures itself, either via a letter to the same newspaper or otherwise." The situation was not one in which "a teacher has carelessly made fale statements about matters so closely related to the day-to-day operations of the schools."[23]

Finally, with respect to the allegation that Pickering's letter impaired the efficient operation of the school system—including the need for faculty discipline, the need to maintain harmony among coworkers, and the need to maintain the working relationship between Pickering and his nominal superiors—the Court pointed out that the board hearing produced no evidence to support such claims. On the contrary, "Pickering's letter was greeted by everyone but its main target, the board, with massive apathy and total disbelief." The board could conceivably have argued that Pickering's letter was detrimental to the ability of the school district to raise additional revenues for its athletic programs. But since Pickering's letter was published after voters defeated a tax increase proposition, the letter could not have adversely affected the board's ability to raise tax revenues. In the Court's view, the school board failed to demonstrate the presence of vital state interest.

*Pickering* only focused on matters of public concern. It did not address the constitutional status of criticisms or expressive conduct made in pursuit of personal or private interests—speech that is of no public consequence. In *Connick v. Myers* (1983),[24] which clarified this question, the Court held that the First Amendment would not protect expressive conduct motivated by a personal interest such as insubordination. Sheila Myers, an assistant district attorney for the city of New Orleans, was notified that, despite her objections, she would be transferred to a different section of criminal court. She then prepared a questionnaire on her concerns, seeking other employees' views on office transfer policy and matters such as morale, the need for a grievance committee, and the level of confidence in supervisors. The questionnaire also included one item asking whether employees felt pressured to work in political campaigns. Calling the survey an act of insubordination, the district attorney, Harry Connick, summarily terminated Myers' employment. On certiorari, the Supreme Court held that while one questionnaire item touched upon matters of public concern, the overall questionnaire did not fall into the category of public concern but reflected "one employee's dissatisfaction with a transfer and an attempt to turn that displeasure into a cause celebre." "Whether an employee's speech addresses a matter of public concern," said the Court, "must be determined by the content, form and context of a given statement as revealed by the whole record."[25] It went on to note that "[t]he limited First Amendment interest involved does not require that [the supervisor] tolerate action which he reasonably believes would disrupt the office, undermine his authority, and destroy close working relationships."[26]

In 1987, in *Rankin v. McPherson*,[27] the Supreme Court expanded *Pickering's* public domain argument while applying dictum in *Connick v. Myers* calling for contextual consideration of the expression in issue. Ardith McPherson, a probationary clerical employee in the office of the constable of Harris County, Texas, was summarily dismissed by Constable Rankin for remarking to a coworker, after hearing of an attempt on President Reagan's life, "If they go for him again, I hope they get him." As Justice Powell quipped in his concurring opinion, "It is not easy to understand how this case has assumed constitutional dimensions and reached the Supreme Court of the United States."[28] In the course of analysis, the Court provided a further insight on the outer limit of First Amendment rights.

McPherson's testified conversation went as follows:

Q: What did you say?
A: I said I felt that that would happen sooner or later.
Q: Okay. And what did Lawrence say?
A: Lawrence said, yeah, agreeing with me.
Q: Okay. Now, when you—after Lawrence spoke, then what was your next comment?
A: Well, we were talking—it's a wonder why they did that. I felt like it would be a black person that did that, because I feel like most of my kind is on welfare and CETA, and they use medicaid, and at the time, I was thinking that's what it was. . . . But then after I said that, and then Lawrence said, yea, welfare and CETA. I said, shoot, if they go for him again, I hope they get him.

Could this speech be characterized as a matter of public concern? Applying *Connick*, the majority believed that it could be so characterized. Note that in *Connick*, the Court emphasized that an employee's speech is determined by the content, form, and context of a given statement, as revealed by the whole record. Applying this rule, the Court concluded that McPherson's "statement was made in the course of a conversation addressing the policies of the President's administration. It came on the heels of a news bulletin regarding what is certainly a matter of heightened public attention: an attempt on the life of the President."[29] The Court stated that "debate on public issues . . . may well include vehement, caustic, and sometimes unpleasantly sharp attacks on government and public officials."

Applying *Pickering*'s criteria, the Court concluded that "While McPherson's statement was made at the workplace, there is no evidence that it interfered with the efficient functioning of the office. . . . Nor was there any danger that McPherson had discredited the office by making her statement in public," since her remark was made in an area to which there was no public access. As to the argument that no law enforcement agency is required by the First Amendment to permit one of its employees to "ride with the cops and cheer for the robbers," the Court responded, "The burden of caution employees bear with respect to the words they speak will vary with the extent of authority and public accountability the employee's role entails."[30] "Where, as here," observed the Court, "an employee serves no confidential, policymaking, or public contact role, the danger to the agency's successful function from that employee's private speech is minimal."[31] From this perspective, Constable Rankin "failed to demonstrate a state interest that would outweigh McPherson's First Amendment rights."

## THE HATCH ACT AND
## PARTISAN POLITICAL ACTIVITY

A major impetus to the 19th century civil service reform was a reaction to the spoils politics in which civil service positions were used as an instrument to advance the interests of political parties. The first civil service reform act, the Pendleton Act of 1883, provided that "no person in said service has any right to use his official authority or influence to coerce the political action of any person or body."[32] The act authorized the president to promulgate regulations to enforce this provision. Under this authority, the Civil Service Commission, in 1907, set forth the following:

> No person in the Executive civil service shall use his official authority or influence for the purpose of interfering with an election or affecting the result thereof. Persons who, by the provisions of these rules are in the competitive classified service, while retaining the right to vote as they please and to express privately their opinions on all political subjects, shall take no active part in political management or in political campaigns.[33]

Implementation of this rule resulted in a body of case law based on thousands of cases. Drawing from this case law, in 1940, Congress enacted the Hatch Act, which has been amended many times over the years. The most controversial part of the act is Section 9 (a) and (b). The original legislation reads as follows:

> It shall be unlawful for any person employed in the executive branch of the Federal Government, or any agency or department thereof, to use his official authority or influence for the purpose of interfering with an election or affecting the result thereof. No officer or employee in the executive branch of the Federal Government, or any agency or department thereof, except a part-time officer or part-time employee without compensation or with nominal compensation serving in connection with the existing war effort, or other than in any capacity relating to the procurement or manufacture of war material, shall take any active part in political management or in political campaigns. All such persons shall retain the right to vote as they may choose and to express their opinions on all political subjects and candidates. For the purposes of this section the term "officer" or "employee" shall not be construed to include (1) the President and Vice President of the United States; (2) persons whose compensation is paid from the

appropriation for the office of the President; (3) heads and assistant heads of executive departments; (4) officers who are appointed by the President, by and with the advice and consent of the Senate, and who determine policies to be pursued by the United States in its relations with foreign powers or in the nationwide administration of Federal laws (b) Any person violating the provisions of this section shall be immediately removed from the position or office held by him, and thereafter no part of the funds appropriated by an Act of Congress for such position or office shall be used to pay the compensation of such person.[34]

The constitutionality of the Hatch Act has been challenged on various grounds. Some urged that Section 9(a) (which incorporates a Civil Service Commission disciplinary rule promulgated in 1938) was repugnant to the Constitution and violated the First Amendment rights of public employees as citizens. They argued that public employees should be free to serve their political parties on their own time as private citizens. Others challenged the act on the ground that the language of Section 9(a)—"taking an active part in political management or in political campaigns"—was too vague or overbroad. In either case, the Court maintained consistently that the state has a legitimate interest in restricting public employees' First Amendment freedoms in connection with partisan political activity, that Congress has the authority under the Constitution to forbid federal employees from actively engaging in partisan political activity, and that the definition of political activity provided in the Civil Service Commission's regulations is specific and sufficiently clear.

In 1947, in *United Public Workers of America v. Mitchell*,[35] several employees of the federal government, including a Mr. Poole, argued to the Supreme Court that Section 9(a) unconstitutionally interfered with their First Amendment freedoms. Poole was a Democratic Ward Executive Committeeman in the City of Philadelphia and was politically active in the 1940 general election as a poll worker on election day and paymaster for the services of other party workers. Upon his admission of political activity, the Civil Service Commission, in 1944, ordered his employer, the United States Mint at Philadelphia, to discharge him from the service. Many others, including the United Public Workers of America, joined in the suit seeking a declaratory judgment of the unconstitutionality of Section 9(a). The argument was presented that in discharge of their duties of citizenship, of their right to vote, and in exercise of their constitutional rights to freedom of speech, press, assembly, and the right to engage in political activity, it is important that federal employees engage in certain political activities, such as writing for publication letters and articles in support of candidates for office, soliciting votes, participating in political parades, and canvassing for signatures of others on petitions. Poole, in particular, contended that the Hatch Act and the Civil Service Commission rule could not, without violating the Constitution, be the basis for his dismissal. Poole stated in his affidavit:

> I have for a long time been interested in political activities. Both before and since my employment in the United States Mint, I have taken an active part in political campaigns and political management. In the 28th Ward, 7th Division in the City of Philadelphia I am and have been a Ward Executive Committeeman. In that position I have on many occasions taken an active part in political management and political campaigns. I have visited the residents of my Ward and solicited them to support my party and its candidates; I have acted as a watcher at the polls; I have contributed money to help pay its expenses; I have circulated campaign literature, placed banners and posters in public places, distributed leaflets, assisted in organizing political rallies and assemblies, and have done any and all acts which were asked of me in my capacity as a Ward Executive Commit-teeman. I have engaged in these activities both before and after my employment in the United States Mint. I intend to continue to engage in these activities *on my own time* as a private citizen, openly, freely, and without concealment.[36]

The Court acknowledged that to an extent, Poole's political rights were interfered with by the Hatch Act and the Civil Service Commission rule. It maintained, however, that "it is accepted constitutional doctrine that these fundamental human rights are not absolute. . . . The essential rights of the First Amendment in some instances are subject to the elemental need for order without which the guarantees of civil rights to others would be a mockery."[37] In this perspective, the "Court must balance the extent of the guarantees of freedom against a congressional enactment to protect a democratic society against the supposed evil of political partisanship by classified employees of government." The Court went on to stress that partisan political activity by classified public employees can be a "material threat to the democratic system," so Congress and the president have the responsibility to run an efficient public service. "If in their judgment," declared the Court, "efficiency may be best obtained by prohibiting active participation by classified employees in politics as party officers or workers, the Court sees no constitutional objection."[38]

Concerning the constitutionality of the Hatch Act on which the Court was asked to rule, the *United Public Workers* Court invoked the established principle that federal courts do not give advisory opinions and refused to respond. In *Civil Service Commission v. National Association of Letter Carriers* (1973),[39] the Supreme Court took up the issue where *United Public Workers* left off. In this case, several federal employees, and certain local Republican and Democratic committees, filed a complaint on behalf of themselves and all federal employees that Section 9(a) of the Hatch Act was unconstitutional on the ground that the language in Section 9(a) was unconstitutionally vague and overbroad. The district court initially agreed with the complainants, but on certiorari, the Supreme Court, in a six to three decision, rejected the lower court holding, thereby letting *United Public Workers* stand. Arguing that, historically, an actively partisan governmental personnel presents a threat to the public service, the Court declared, once again, that Congress and the president have the constitutional responsibility to develop an efficient public service. Prohibition of partisan political activity by classified employees would be within the ambit of this responsibility.

To the extent that government has a legitimate interest in regulating the free speech of its civil servants, a balance must be struck "between the interest of the [employee] as a citizen, in commenting upon matters of public concern and the interest of the [government] as an employer, in promoting the efficiency of the public service it performs through its employees." Applying the balancing standard, the Court concluded that the Hatch Act's prohibition [would] "reduce the hazards to fair and efficient government."[40]

The Court also rejected the claim that Section 9(a) was "both unconstitutionally vague and totally overbroad." When working on Section 9(a), Congress relied on a body of law the Civil Service Commission had developed over three decades on a case-by-case basis under Civil Service Rule I adopted in 1907. Pursuant to the 1940 statute and the original mandate, the Court noted that the commission, in 1970, had further clarified the meaning of political activity, detailing those acts that are forbidden and those that are permitted by the Hatch Act. For example, the revised regulations provide:

*Permissible activities* (Section 733.111):
(a) All employees are free to engage in political activity to the widest extent consistent with the restrictions imposed by law and this subpart. Each employee retains the right to—
    (1) Register and vote in any election;
    (2) Express his opinion as an individual privately and publicly on political subjects and candidates;

(3) Display a political picture, sticker, badge, or button;
(4) Participate in the nonpartisan activities of a civic, community, social, labor, or professional organization, or of a similar organization;
(5) Be a member of a political party or other political organization and participate in its activities to the extent consistent with law;
(6) Attend a political convention, rally, fund-raising function; or other political gathering;
(7) Sign a political petition as an individual;
(8) Make a financial contribution to a political party or organization;
(9) Take an active part, as a candidate or in support of a candidate, in a nonpartisan election;
(10) Be politically active in connection with a question which is not specifically identified with a political party, such as a constitutional amendment, referendum, approval of a municipal ordinance or any other question or issue of a similar character;
(11) Serve as an election judge or clerk, or in a similar position to perform nonpartisan duties as prescribed by State or local law; and
(12) Otherwise participate fully in public affairs, except as prohibited by law, in a manner which does not materially compromise his efficiency or integrity as an employee or the neutrality, efficiency, or integrity of his agency.

*"Prohibited Activities* (Section 733.122):
(a) An employee may not take an active part in political management or in a political campaign, except as permitted by this subpart.
(b) Activities prohibited by paragraph (a) of this section include but are not limited to—
    (1) Serving as an officer of a political party, a member of a National, State, or local committee of a political party, an officer or member of a committee of a partisan political club, or being a candidate for any of these positions;
    (2) Organizing or reorganizing a political party organization or political club;
    (3) Directly or indirectly soliciting, receiving, collecting, handling, disbursing, or accounting for assessments, contributions, or other funds for a partisan political purpose;
    (4) Organizing, selling tickets to, promoting, or actively participating in a fund-raising activity of a partisan candidate, political party, or political club;
    (5) Taking an active part in managing the political campaign of a partisan candidate for public office or political party office;
    (6) Becoming a partisan candidate for, or campaigning for, an elective public office;
    (7) Soliciting votes in support of or in opposition to a partisan candidate for public office or political party office;
    (8) Acting as recorder, watcher, challenger, or similar officer at the polls on behalf of a political party or partisan candidate;
    (9) Driving voters to the polls on behalf of a political party or partisan candidate;
    (10) Endorsing or opposing a partisan candidate for public office or political party office in a political advertisement, a broadcast, campaign literature, or similar material;
    (11) Serving as a delegate, alternate, or proxy to a political party convention;

(12) Addressing a convention, caucus, rally, or similar gathering of a political party in support of or in opposition to a partisan candidate for public office or political party office; and

(13) initiating or circulating a partisan nominating petition.[41]

In The Court's view, these regulations were "wholly legitimate descendants" of the Hatch Act of 1940, and they could be accepted as "the current and, in most respects, the longstanding interpretations of the statute by the agency charged with its interpretation and enforcement."[42] The Court acknowledged that some prohibitions such as partisan endorsement or speech making may be constitutionally overbroad. But the Court believed that "its task is not to destroy the Act if [it] can, but to construe it, if it is consistent with the will of Congress, so as to comport with constitutional limitations."[43]

## PATRONAGE APPOINTMENT AND DISMISSAL

Closely related to the issue of regulating civil servants' partisan political activity is the practice of patronage—basing personnel decisions (hiring, promotion, transfer, and dismissal) on party affiliation. It is important to remember that the civil service reform movement under the Pendleton Act—and subsequent civil service reform laws in federal and state governments—was not intended to eliminate patronage practice. It aimed to eliminate patronage practice within the newly established competitive civil service system. This has left all noncompetitive positions open to patronage practice, including federal judgeships and all political (non-merit) appointments. It is here that much of the case law has focused. The First Amendment declares that "Congress shall make no law respecting . . . the right of the people peaceably to assemble." The question is whether a government employee not protected by the merit system can be discharged on the ground of his partisan political affiliation. Although the Court has recognized that, under certain circumstances, party affiliation may be an acceptable requirement for some types of government employment, the Court has been very careful about where to draw the line.

In *Elrod v. Burns* (1976),[44] the Court was presented with a question whether nonmerit employees who are not in policy-making or confidential positions can be discharged without violating the Constitution solely on the basis of their political beliefs or party affiliation. This question arose when Richard Elrod, newly elected sheriff of Cook County, Illinois, terminated several employees in the sheriff's office because they were not members of the Democratic party and had failed to obtain the sponsorship of party leaders. Among those dismissed were the chief deputy of the Process Division; a bailiff and security guard at the Juvenile Court, and an employee in the office. Another employee, a process server, was threatened with discharge for the same reason. It should be noted that the county had a long-standing practice that newly elected officeholders were permitted to replace incumbent nonmerit employees on patronage grounds. The Cook County Sheriff's Office employed approximately three thousand people of whom about half were protected by the merit system. Ironically, John Burns and others in this class action were the beneficiaries of the very patronage practice they were challenging.

The Court reached a judgment, in a plurality opinion, in which Justice Stewart cast a crucial swing vote concurring in the judgment. The Court concluded that patronage dismissal severely restricted political belief and association protected by the First Amendment and that government may not, without seriously inhibiting First Amendment rights, force a public employee to relinquish his right to political association as the price of holding a public job. It observed that an employee who is the member of an outgoing party is at risk of losing his employment if he maintains his party affiliation. If, just for the sake of keeping his job, the employee would give a pledge of allegiance to another party, that would mean a compromise of his true belief.

Having said that, the plurality, per Justice Brennan, acknowledged the Court's previous position set forth in *United Public Workers* that First Amendment rights are not absolute and that they may be constrained upon the showing of a legitimate governmental interest. In this case, "[the] encroachment cannot be justified upon a mere showing of a legitimate state interest. The interest advanced must be paramount, one of vital importance, and the burden is on the government to show the existence of such an interest."[45] "Moreover, it is not enough that the means chosen in furtherance of the interest be rationally related to that end." The means chosen must be "closely drawn to avoid unnecessary abridgment," that is, "least restrictive of freedom of belief and association in achieving that end."[46]

Against these criteria the Court looked at three arguments of state interest advanced by Elrod, including efficiency, accountability, and the preservation of the democratic process. The Court did not think that the wholesale replacement of large numbers of public employees every time political office changes hands would increase efficiency. Nor would it necessarily promote the ideals of a representative government in that those in non-policy-making positions have "only limited responsibility and are therefore not in a position to thwart the goals of the in-party."[47] Nor was the Court persuaded that patronage dismissals would indisputably contribute to the preservation of the democratic process. The Court observed, "The process functions as well without the practice, perhaps even better, for patronage dismissals clearly also retard that process . . . [because they] can result in the entrenchment of one or a few parties to the exclusion of others."[48]

The Court concluded that patronage dismissals severely restrict political belief and association. While government needs to insure that policies that the electorate has sanctioned are effectively implemented, the Court maintained that this interest can be better satisfied by limiting patronage dismissals to policy-making positions. If patronage dismissals are to be limited to policy-making positions, where should the line be drawn between policy-making and non-policy-making positions? Initially the Court left the burden of drawing the line on the hiring authority. Later, in *Branti v. Finkel* (1980),[49] the Court considered this question again.

In *Branti*, the Court, in a six to three decision, established that the hiring authority must demonstrate that "party affiliation is an appropriate requirement for the effective performance of the public office involved." This is because "it is not always easy to determine whether a position is one in which political affiliation is a legitimate factor to be considered." The Court believed that "under some circumstances, a position may be appropriately considered political even though it is neither confidential nor policymaking in character." "It is equally clear," emphasized the Court, "that party affiliation is not necessarily relevant to every policymaking or confidential position." To illustrate the point, the Court, per Justice Stevens, offered:

If a state's election laws require that precincts be supervised by two election judges of different parties, a republican judge could be legitimately discharged solely for changing his party registration. That conclusion would not depend on any finding that the job involved participation in policy decisions or access to confidential information. Rather, it could simply rest on the fact that party membership was essential to the discharge of the employee's governmental responsibilities.

It is equally clear that party affiliation is not necessarily relevant to every policymaking or confidential position. The coach of a state university's football team formulates policy, but no one could seriously claim that republicans make better coaches than democrats, or vice versa, no matter which party is in control of the state government. On the other hand, it is equally clear that the governor of a State may appropriately believe that the official duties of various assistants who help him write speeches, explain his views to the press, or communicate with the legislature cannot be performed effectively unless those persons share his political beliefs and party commitments.[50]

The case in *Branti* involved county assistant public defenders. They were Republicans and were about to be terminated when the county became controlled by Democrats. The Democrat-controlled county legislature appointed Brandi to be the county public defender; Branti immediately began issuing termination notices to assistant public defenders on the grounds of their affiliation with the Republican party. The Court held that, given the nature of the assistant public defenders position, "whatever policy-making occurs in the public defender's office must relate to the needs of the individual clients, and not to any partisan political interests."[51] Failing to demonstrate any overriding state interest, the Court ruled that Rockland County could not terminate its assistant public defenders without violating the First and Fourteenth Amendments.

Both *Elrod* and *Branti* dealt only with patronage dismissals. However, patronage practice is not limited to partisan appointment or dismissal; it may cover a wide range of personnel decisions, including promotion, job transfer, layoff, and recall. The question remained as to whether the First Amendment protection would extend to patronage practices other than dismissal, or only to personnel action that is the "substantial equivalent of a dismissal." In *Rutan v. Republican Party of Illinois* (1990),[52] the Court invented a new aphorism: "To the victor belong only those spoils that may be constitutionally obtained." And it concluded that "promotions, transfers, and recalls after layoffs based on political affiliation or support are an impermissible infringement on the First Amendment rights of public employees."[53] Rejecting the argument proffered by the Seventh Circuit Court of Appeals that "only those employment decisions that are the substantial equivalent of a dismissal violate a public employees' right under the First Amendment," the U.S. Supreme Court insisted that "[e]mployees who find themselves in dead-end positions due to their political backgrounds are adversely affected."[54] Similarly, "[e]mployees who do not compromise their beliefs stand to lose the considerable increases in pay and job satisfaction attendant to promotions, the hours and maintenance expenses that are consumed by long daily commutes, and even their jobs if they are not rehired after a temporary layoff. These are significant penalties and are imposed for the exercise of rights guaranteed by the First Amendment."[55]

The Rutan complaint originated from the personnel policy of Illinois under Governor James Thompson. On November 12, 1980, the governor issued an executive order announcing a hiring freeze for all public employment positions under his control. The order affected approximately sixty thousand state positions, of which more than five thousand became available each year as a result of resignations, retirements, deaths, expansion, and reorganization. The order prohibited state agencies from hiring any employee, filling any vacancy, creating any new position, or taking any similar action without the governor's "express permission" via the Governor's Office of Personnel. The Governor's Office, then, allegedly screened all agency requests based on "whether the applicant voted in Republican primaries in past election years, whether the applicant has provided financial or other support to the Republican Party and its candidates, whether the applicant has promised to join and work for the Republican Party in the future, and whether the applicant has the support of Republican Party officials at state or local levels."[56] The *Rutan* plantiffs alleged that they had been repeatedly denied promotions, not recalled after layoffs, or not hired because they lacked Republican credentials.

Applying the *Elrod* test that "conditioning hiring decisions on political belief and association plainly constitutes an unconstitutional condition, unless the government has a vital interest in doing so," the Court determined that no such interest was present in this case, in patronage hiring, promotions, transfers, or recalls.

## SUMMARY AND CONCLUSION

Nearly a century after the adoption of the Constitution, the nation finally accepted a modern civil service system based on merit, thereby doing away with the spoils system. This change, however, did not completely transform the public employment relationship to conform with the Constitution. Another seventy-five years elapsed before the public service was "constitutionalized." In the interim, public service was considered a privilege, with public employees serving at the pleasure of the government as employer. Once the public service was brought within the constitutional framework, the legal environment of the public sector personnel management was fundamentally transformed—from the primacy of state interest as a guidepost in management to that of a balance between state interest and the rights conferred upon public employees as individuals.

The case law principles developed under the new paradigm hold that freedoms guaranteed by the Constitution are not absolute and may be constitutionally subject to restriction when circumstances dictate. In such cases, the Court has been insistent that the interest of the state be of paramount importance, not simply a matter of convenience. Moreover, the means selected for such restriction should be narrowly tailored—not vague or overbroad—to serve the stated purpose. In sum, the Court requires a two-prong test of a state action subjecting it to strict scrutiny, a standard of judicial review that holds closely or strictly to the letter of the Constitution.

Not all justices on the Court, however, agree with the application of the strict scrutiny standard to the public employment relationship. The dissenting justices have been arguing that the Court should apply a lower level of scrutiny in weighing the balance between state interests and individual rights. Instead of requiring the standards of vital state interests and narrowly-tailored means, they have been in favor of a reasonableness test.[57] The reasonableness test would hold that First Amendment restrictions may be considered valid if they bear a rational connection to the purpose they serve. The reason for this lower standard is that, as Justice Scalia maintained in his dissent in *Rutan v. Republican Party of Illinois*, "[t]he restrictions that the Constitution places upon the government in its capacity as lawmaker . . . are not the same as the restrictions that it places upon the government in its capacity as employer." According to Scalia, with whom Chief Justice Rehnquist and Justices Kennedy and O'Connor joined, when dealing with its own employees, government as employer ought to be recognized "as proprietor to manage its internal operations."[58]

This view returns full circle to the private sector model of personnel administration that had been applied earlier in the public sector, and subsequently discarded in the 1960s. Inasmuch as the Court decision is ultimately a function of a majority vote, however, a possibility always exists that the pendulum may swing in either direction depending on who sits on the bench. Today, considering the composition of the Rehnquist Court—justices supporting the state interest over individual rights constitute a large majority[59]—it is not inconceivable that the pendulum may swing to the side of state interests.

## NOTES

1. Arch Dotson, "The Emerging Doctrine of Privilege in Public Employment," *Public Administration Review* 15, no. 2 (Spring 1955), 77–88).

2. *McAuliffe v. Mayor of City of Bedford*, 155 Mass. 216 (1892).

3. Frank J. Sorauf, "The Silent Revolution in Patronage," *Public Administration Review* (Winter 1960), 28–34.

4. Herbert Agaar, *The Price of Union* (Boston: Houghton Mifflin, 1966). See especially chapter 24, "Grantism and Congressional Policy-Making," pp. 485–508.

5. Ibid., 533.

6. *Bailey v. Richardson*, 86 U.S. App. D.C. 248, 261 (1950).

7. *Adler v. Board of Education*, 342 U.S. 485 (1952).

8. Ibid., 492.

9. Ibid., 493.

10. *Keyishian v. Board of Regents*, 385 U.S. 589 (1967).

11. Ibid., 603.

12. Ibid., 604.

13. Ibid., 601.

14. Ibid., 607.

15. The doctrine of privilege has been rejected in several cases, including *Wieman v. Updegraff*, 344 U.S. 183 (1952); *Slochower v. Board of Education*, 350 U.S. 551 (1955); *Cramp v. Board of Public Instruction*, 368 U.S. 278 (1961); *Shelton v. Tucker*, 364 U.S. 479 (1960); and *Torasco v. Watkins*, 367 U.S. 488 (1960).

16. David Rosenbloom, "Public Personnel Administration and the Constitution: An Emergent Approach," *Public Administration Review* 35, no. 1 (January/February 1975), 54.

17. *Pickering v. Board of Education*, 391 U.S. 563 (1968).

18. Ibid., 568.

19. Ibid., 574.

20. Ibid., 569.

21. See *New York Times v. Sullivan*, 376 U.S. 254 (1964); and *Garrison v. Louisiana*, 379 U.S. 64 (1964).

22. Rosenbloom, "Public Personnel Administration," 54.

23. *Pickering*, 572.

24. *Connick v. Myers*, 461 U.S. 138 (1983).

25. Ibid., 1690.

26. Ibid., 1694.

27. *Rankin v. McPherson*, 483 U.S. 378 (1987).

28. Ibid., 392.

29. Ibid., 386.

30. Ibid., 390.

31. Ibid., 391.

32. Section 2 (6) of the Civil Service Act of 1883.

33. Section 1 of Rule I of the Civil Service Rules, 3 Fed. Reg. 1525.

34. 53 Stat. 1147, 1148; 54 Stat. 767; 56 Stat. 181.

35. *United Public Workers of America v. Mitchell*, 330 U.S. 75 (1947).

36. Ibid., 91, see also footnote 23.

37. Ibid., 95.

38. Ibid., 99.

39. *Civil Service Commission v. National Association of Letter Carriers*, 413 U.S. 548 (1973).

40. Ibid., 565.

41. CFR pt. 733 (1970).

42. *Letter Carriers*, 575.

43. Ibid., 571.

44. *Elrod v. Burns*, 427 U.S. 347 (1976).

45. Ibid., 362.

46. Ibid., 363.
47. Ibid., 367.
48. Ibid., 369.
49. *Branti v. Finkel*, 445 U.S. 507 (1980).
50. Ibid., 518.
51. Ibid., 519.
52. *Rutan v. Republican Party of Illinois*, 58 LW 4872 (1990).
53. Ibid., 4875.
54. Ibid.
55. Ibid.
56. Ibid., 4873.
57. See Justice Scalia's dissenting opinion in *Rutan*, 4880–4886.
58. Ibid., 4881.
59. The retirement of Justices Brennan and Marshall—the two pronounced liberal justices—during the past year, leaves the Court completely under the dominance of conservatives who are in favor of state interests. See also William C. Louthan, *The United States Supreme Court* (Englewood Cliffs, N.J.: Prentice Hall, 1991), 220–233.

# 4

---

# *Equal Employment Opportunity and Public Policy*

Phil Bazemore, a black agent in the Agricultural Extension Service at North Carolina State University, had just turned 51 in 1972 when Congress amended Title VII of the Civil Rights Act of 1964 to make it applicable to public sector employment. The amendment provided an opportunity for him and his colleagues similarly situated in the Extension Service to redress a long-standing pay discrimination complaint that they had with the Extension Service. They promptly filed a lawsuit against the university in United States District Court for the Eastern District of North Carolina, alleging that they were systematically paid less than their white counterparts for performing the same work under the same job titles and job descriptions and with the same, if not more, experience; they also alleged they had been routinely passed over for promotion. They argued that the university policy and practice were in violation of the Equal Protection Clause of the Fourteenth Amendment and the Equal Employment Opportunity Act of 1972. They demanded that their pay be brought to par with their white colleagues. The university rejected the demand, arguing that it had already corrected the past discriminatory practices and that it could not be responsible for the effects of discrimination that had occurred prior to the enactment of Title VII as amended in 1972. This meant that the university would not be responsible for the so-called "pre-act" discrimination. District Judge Franklin T. DuPree agreed with the university's interpretation of Title VII and denied the claims sought by Bazemore and his fellow plaintiffs.

Bazemore appealed, but the Court of Appeals for the Fourth Circuit did not think that Bazemore's statistical evidence, supported by multiple regression analysis, made out a prima facie case of discrimination, the first step in Title VII litigation. Moreover, the court of appeals upheld the district court ruling, stating that the present pay disparity was due to the pre-act treatment and that the Extension Service was not responsible for the effects of pre-act discrimination within the meaning of Title VII. Bazemore then applied to the U.S. Supreme Court for certiorari, and the Court granted a writ to review the case.

Meanwhile, many in the plaintiff class had died. One day Bazemore visited D. O. Ivey, a fellow plaintiff who was in the hospital dying of lung cancer. Gasping for breath, Ivey whispered to Bazemore, "Don't give up . . . fight harder than ever . . . because those guys don't ever intend to do justice to black people." Bazemore looked down at his friend and saw his face full of anger—"An anger," Bazemore later confessed, "so intense that Ivey was almost crying." Ivey did not live long enough to hear the good news. In 1987, six years after his death, the Supreme Court reached a unanimous opinion holding, "Each week's pay check that delivers less to a black than to a similarly situated white is a wrong actionable under Title VII . . . regardless of the fact that this pattern began prior to the effective date of Title VII." It concluded that "[t]he Court of Appeals plainly erred in holding that the pre-Act discriminatory difference in salaries did not have to be eliminated."[1]

The Court remanded the case for a new trial by DuPree—the same judge who vindictively vowed, "I'm not going to be any more generous to civil rights plaintiffs than I absolutely have to be."[2] Feeling that bureaucracy might outlive him, Bazemore lamented to an interviewer:

> I don't think you're capable of understanding the kind and depth of bitterness we have. If you have the opportunity to take a time bomb and blow up all of the things connected with this lawsuit, you'd about to go to that extent. This is a degree of bitterness I'll take to my grave. There's no way out of it.[3]

It is possible that the court battle might outlive Bazemore. What is at stake in *Bazemore* is the principle of equal employment opportunity and the experience that shapes this principle. The issue raised by Bazemore is one of pay discrimination, particularly as it relates to the continuing effect of past discrimination, or more precisely, to discrimination that predates the enactment of Title VII of the Civil Rights Act of 1964, as amended in 1972. The issues of discrimination are numerous, including

the problems of organizational membership, hiring, on-the-job treatment, promotion, and transfer. At the core of the legal process are three
principle questions: (1) what constitutes unlawful discrimination, (2)
what evidence is required to prove this unlawful discrimination, and (3)
what remedies are available under the law? The present chapter examines
these questions.

What constitutes unlawful discrimination is problematic in that, for the
most part, it involves the interpretation of law. In the United States it is a
matter of constitutional law involving the Fifth and Fourteenth Amendments of the Constitution and of statutory construction relative to civil
rights statutes, including Section 1983 of the Civil Rights Act of 1871 and
Title VII of the Civil Rights Act of 1964, as amended in 1972. The
Fourteenth Amendment provides no easy solution to the problem of racial
discrimination. In fact, it presents both an American ideal and a paradox.
We look at this paradox first.

## EQUAL PROTECTION OF THE LAWS

Perhaps most dramatic in the history of American constitutional development is the evolution of the Equal Protection Clause of the Fourteenth
Amendment, which literally guarantees equal protection of all under the
laws. For eighty years after its adoption in 1868, however, the promise of
equal protection was systematically thwarted for blacks and other racial
minorities. Equal protection was denied in employment, education, housing, public transportation, and public accommodations. Blacks and other
racial minorities were equal before the laws, but as the Supreme Court
interpreted the Equal Protection Clause, they had no constitutional right
to commingle socially.[4] In 1871, three years after the ratification of the
Fourteenth Amendment, Congress enacted the Civil Rights Act, imposing
civil liability for state and local governmental bodies (and officials)
involved in the deprivation of rights guaranteed by the Constitution and
other laws; but this, too, was left dormant for the next hundred years.[5]
Meaningful progress toward civil rights for blacks and other racial minorities did not begin until 1954 when the U.S. Supreme Court in *Brown v.
Board of Education*[6] reversed the so-called "separate but equal doctrine"
established in *Plessy v. Ferguson* in 1896.

On June 7, 1892, Mr. Plessy, who had a one-eighth proportion of African
blood, boarded a section of a train in New Orleans designated only for
whites. Another section of the train, which was en route to Covington,
Louisiana, was designated for blacks, exclusively. Louisiana law provided,
"All railway companies carrying passengers in their coaches in this State

shall provide *equal but separate* accommodations for the white and colored races . . . and [no] person or persons shall be admitted to occupy seats in coaches other than the ones assigned to them on account of the race they belong to (emphasis added)." The statute also provided that "the officers of such passenger trains shall have power and are hereby required to assign each passenger to the coach or compartment used for the race to which such passenger belongs; and any passenger insisting on going into a coach or compartment to which by race he does not belong, shall be liable to a fine of twenty-five dollars, or in lieu thereof to imprisonment for a period of not more than twenty days in the parish prison." Plessy, whose appearance was indistinguishable from whites, took a vacant seat in a coach designated for whites only. The conductor ordered him to vacate the seat, and Plessy refused. With the aid of a police officer, the conductor forcibly ejected Plessy and hurried him off to the parish jail.

Plessy was tried in the criminal district court. He argued, through counsel, that the Louisiana statute was null and void because it was in violation of the Thirteenth and Fourteenth Amendments of the U.S. Constitution. The trial court, and later the state supreme court, held that the statute was not in conflict with the Constitution. Thereafter, Plessy filed a petition to the U.S. Supreme Court for a writ of certiorari, which the Court granted.

In the Supreme Court, Plessy argued that refusing accommodations to colored people could be regarded as imposing a badge of slavery or servitude. Announcing the opinion of the Court, Justice Brown said, "A statute which implies merely a legal distinction between the white and colored races—a distinction which is found in the color of the two races, and which must always exist so long as white men are distinguished from the other race by color—has no tendency to destroy the legal equality of the two races, or reestablish a state of involuntary servitude."[7]

With regard to the equal protection claim *Plessy* was making, the Court maintained that "the object of the 14th Amendment was . . . to enforce the absolute equality of the two races before the law, but in the nature of things it could not have been intended to abolish distinctions based on color, or to enforce *social*, as distinguished from *political equality*, or a commingling of the two races upon terms unsatisfactory to either (emphasis added)."[8] "Laws permitting, and even requiring, their separation in places where they are liable to be brought into contact," Brown stated, "do not necessarily imply the inferiority of either race to the other and have been generally, if not universally recognized, as within the competency of the state legislatures in the exercise of their police power." To buttress this point, interestingly, the justice used the example of education. He pointed out, "The most common instance of this is connected with the establishment of separate schools for white and colored children, which has been held to be a valid exercise of the legislative power by even courts of States [including Massachusetts and District of Columbia] where the political rights of the colored race have been longest and most earnestly enforced." Likewise, continued the justice, laws forbidding the intermarriage of the two races and laws providing separate theaters and railway carriages have been recognized as within the police power of the state.

The *Plessy* decision was not without powerful dissent. Justice Harlan Jr. disagreed with the Court majority challenging:

> If a State can prescribe, as a rule of civil conduct, that whites and blacks shall not travel as passengers in the same railroad coach, why may it not so regulate the use of the streets of its cities and towns as to compel white citizens to keep on one side of a street and black citizens to keep on the other? Why may it not, upon like grounds, punish whites and blacks who ride together in street cars or in open vehicles on a public road or street? Why may it not require sheriffs to assign whites to one side of a court-room and blacks to the other? Why may it not also prohibit the commingling of the two races in the galleries of legislative halls or in public assemblages convened for the consideration of the political questions of the day?[9]

Justice Harlan argued that "regulations of the kind they suggest would be unreasonable, and could not, therefore, stand before the law." He admonished the Court that whites were the dominant race in this country, and therefore in prestige, achievement, education, wealth, and power. And he declared, "So, I doubt not, it will continue to be for all time, if it remains true to its great heritage and holds fast to the principles of constitutional liberty." "But in view of the Constitution, in the eye of the law," emphasized Justice Harlan, "there is in this country no superior, dominant, ruling class of citizens," and "our Constitution is color-blind."[10]

And yet, the Court majority agreed in *Plessy* to "constitutionalize" racial segregation. As Chief Justice Warren painstakingly acknowledged more than a half-century later in *Brown v. Board of Education*—in which *Plessy* was finally overturned—the legislative history of the Fourteenth Amendment is inconclusive with respect to its original intent. So the *Plessy* decision was a product of both common law practice and of the organization of public service at the time. In 1896, many public services, including education, were organized by the private sector and remained outside the purview of the Equal Protection Clause. Now that these services are increasingly provided by the public sector, they have come under the protection of the Fourteenth Amendment. In *Plessy*, Justice Brown only used education as an example to substantiate the validity of the separate but equal doctrine because, as Brown noted, even Congress passed a law for the District of Columbia that provided separate educational facilities for black children and white children, respectively.

The doctrine of separate but equal was attacked in several lawsuits during the 1930s and 1940s, but it was in *Brown v. Board of Education* that its constitutionality was directly challenged. Black children of elementary school age residing in Topeka, Kansas; Prince Edward County, Virginia; and New Castle County, Deleware sought to obtain admission to the public schools of their respective communities on a nonsegregated basis. In each instance, the children were denied admission to schools attended by white children pursuant to laws requiring or permitting segregation according to race. In all of the cases except Delaware, federal district courts denied relief, relying on the *Plessy* doctrine. What was unique about the *Brown* case was that the plaintiffs, as a class, were able to structure their claim demonstrating that the black schools and the white schools were substantially equal with respect to buildings, curricula, qualifications and salaries of teachers, and other tangible factors, with the only difference being segregation on racial lines. The plaintiffs insisted, "The segregation of children in public schools solely on the basis of race, even though physical facilities and other 'tangible' factors may be equal, [would] deprive the children of the minority group of equal educational opportunities."[11]

Leading the unanimous Court, Chief Justice Warren concluded that "in the field of public education the doctrine of 'separate but equal' has no place" and that segregation in public education is "a denial of the equal protection of the laws."[12] The chief justice acknowledged circumstances had changed since the *Plessy* decision and that the black and white schools involved had been equalized in many tangible respects. "Our decision, therefore, cannot turn on merely a comparison of these tangible factors," reasoned the chief justice, adding, "We must look instead to the effect of segregation itself on public education."[13] He went on to declare, "To separate [children in grade and high schools] from others of similar age and qualifications solely because of their race generates a feeling of inferiority as to their status in the community that may affect their hearts and minds in a way unlikely ever to be undone."[14] With these words, the *Brown* Court finally closed the unfortunate chapter of the *Plessy* doctrine.

## EQUAL EMPLOYMENT OPPORTUNITY

The *Brown* decision embraced far-reaching ramifications in race relations in American society, but the scope was narrow in that the focus was on educational opportunity in public schools. What the *Brown* decision accomplished, however, was to open a new vista for civil rights advocates, individually and in groups, to demand that if the ideals of equality as envisioned in the Declaration of Independence and the Constitution were to be realized, equal protection must be expanded from public education to all other governmental activities, including higher education, transportation, housing, health care, employment, parks and recreation, and welfare. More important, it was argued, the principle of equal protection and opportunity must be expanded to the private sector.[15]

In the employment sector, the proponents insisted that the law must go beyond the Civil Rights Act of 1871, Section 1981, which narrowly addresses equal employment opportunity at the point of entry.[16] To be effective it must address a broad sweep of the work environment, including hiring, training, job assignments, transfer, promotion, pay, personal interaction, and layoff, freeing all these aspects from discrimination on account of race, color, sex, religion, and national origin.

In 1964, Congress responded with the passage of the Civil Rights Act, addressing all sectors of the economy—education, public housing, transportation, employment, health care, and welfare. With respect to employment, Title VII, Section 703(a), provided:

It shall be an unlawful employment practice for an employer (meaning private employer) to fail . . . to hire or to discharge any individual, or otherwise discriminate against any individual with respect to his compensation, terms, conditions, or privileges of employment, because of such individual's race, color, religion, sex, or national origin; or to limit, segregate, or classify his employees in any way which would deprive or tend to deprive any individual of employment opportunities or otherwise adversely affect his status as an employee, because of such individual's race, color, religion, sex, or national origin.[17]

In the interest of employers, however, Title VII provided in Section 703(h):

Notwithstanding any other provision of this title, it shall not be an unlawful employment practice . . . for an employer to give and to act upon the results of any professionally developed ability test provided that such test, its administration, or action upon the results is not designed, intended or used to discriminate because of race, color, religion, sex, or national origin.[18]

In 1972, Congress amended Title VII to extend its coverage to public sector employment at the federal, state, and local levels. Title VII also established the Equal Employment Opportunity Commission (EEOC), an independent agency with the authority to enforce the law.

A closer look at Title VII reveals that the language is broad and sweeping yet provides few operational standards by which to guide day-to-day administrative decision making or to help the alleged victims of discrimination to redress their grievances. What specific actions, for instance, may constitute discrimination in violation of Title VII; and how may one go about proving it? And what evidence would be required to survive judicial scrutiny? These questions were left to the judiciary and administrative agencies.

## UNLAWFUL DISCRIMINATION

To remain competitive in the market, employers should be able to discriminate in personnel selection between the competent and the incompetent, the qualified and the unqualified, the risky and the safe—regardless of race. This gives a lot of room for masking the true reasons, however. Some employers may, under the guise of merit, require certain qualifications, say a test score, that have no direct relationship to job performance. Even if a qualifying examination is needed, the way in which the test is structured or administered may negatively affect certain racial groups. Also, many personnel decisions are made not on the basis of objective evaluations but on the basis of subjective evaluations, or at best, a mixture of the two. What types of employment practices is Title VII intended to proscribe?

The Supreme Court began to delineate the issues in 1972 in *Griggs v. Duke Power*, the first major Title VII case. In *Griggs*, the unanimous Court, led by Chief Justice Burger, reached the opinion that Title VII "proscribes not only overt discrimination but also practices that are fair in form, but discriminatory in operation."[19] Employers may be engaged in overt (intentional) discrimination when their personnel selection criteria are racially based (or sex-based) or when the selection process is so structured as to operate against a racial minority. Employers may also be engaged in unlawful discrimination when their employment practices—

even though they are fair in form—produce discriminatory consequences.[20]

Duke Power Company's problem was that it had a history of overt discrimination against its black employees, as it had the black employees locked in the low-paying Labor Department. When the Civil Rights Act was enacted into law in 1964, Duke Power lifted its restrictive policy and allowed blacks to transfer to other higher-paying departments, provided they had a high school diploma. On July 2, 1965, the date on which Title VII became effective, the company quickly added an additional requirement of passing two professionally developed tests: the Wonderlic Personnel Test (a general intelligence test) and the Bennett Mechanical Comprehension Test. Blacks at Duke Power immediately complained that the requirements were not job-related and that they would operate mainly to disqualify blacks—which they alleged was unlawful under Title VII.

The U.S. District Court for the Eastern District of North Carolina dismissed the complaint, holding that while Duke Power had previously practiced a policy of overt racial discrimination, it effectively abandoned it with the adoption of objective tests. The court of appeals agreed with the lower court, confirming that "there was no showing of a discriminatory purpose in the adoption of the diploma and test requirements." The Supreme Court, however, disagreed with the lower courts, insisting that the "objective of Congress in the enactment of Title VII . . . was to achieve equality of employment opportunities and remove barriers that have operated in the past to favor an identifiable group of white employees over other employees."[21] And the Court declared, "Under the Act, practices, procedures, or tests neutral on their face, and even neutral in terms of intent, cannot be maintained if they operate to 'freeze' the statuts quo of prior discriminatory employment practices."[22] It also is immaterial, the Court insisted, whether the diploma or test requirements were adopted with or without any intention to discriminate against black employees. "[G]ood intent or absence of discriminatory intent," said the Court, "does not redeem employment procedures or testing mechanisms that operate as 'built-in headwinds' for minority groups and are unrelated to measuring job capability."[23]

To sum up the key points, Title VII is directed not only at intentional discrimination but more importantly at discriminatory consequences resulting from selection methods that are neutral on their face but discriminatory in operation. With respect to discriminatory consequences (disparate impact), the absence of discriminatory motive (bad faith) is irrelevant. And if the disparate impact had occurred, the employer must show that the selection method has a manifest relationship to the employment in question.

## EVIDENTIARY STANDARDS

If Title VII is directed not only at intentional discrimination but also at adverse impacts, how may one go about proving discrimination? In *McDonnell Douglas Corp. v. Green* (1972)[24] and again in *Texas Department of Community Affairs v. Burdine* (1981),[25] the Court set forth a three-step procedure as well as evidentiary requirements necessary for each step. During the last few years (1988, 1989, and 1990), however, the Court has attempted to reallocate the long-standing evidentiary requirements—particularly with respect to disparate impact theory. The shift places a significantly heavier burden on Title VII claimants. It is necessary, therefore, to examine in detail the evidentiary standards set forth for intentional discrimination (disparate treatment) and adverse impacts (disparate impact), separately. But first, we look at the three-step procedure.

In Title VII litigation the first legal obligation of the plaintiff is to make a prima facie showing (presumption) of discrimination by the preponderance of evidence. The preponderance of evidence is that quantum and type of evidence that is of greater weight or more convincing than the evidence offered in opposition to it (*Black Law Dictionary*). Once a plaintiff has successfully constructed a prima facie case, the burden is shifted to the employer who must produce evidence articulating some legitimate, nondiscriminatory reasons (such as business necessity) for the employer's policy or practice. This is the second step in the process. Assuming that the employer has proffered admissible evidence, the burden of persuasion goes back to the Title VII claimant who, again, must prove by a preponderance of the evidence that the reasons offered by the employer are not the true reasons but a pretext. This is the third and final step in Title VII litigation. Let us examine what particular evidence is required to show disparate treatment and disparate impact, respectively.

### Disparate Treatment Theory

The first step that a plaintiff takes in Title VII litigation under the disparate treatment theory is to raise the presumption of intentional discrimination by a preponderance of the evidence. What is required to show intentional discrimination is evidence that (1) the plaintiff belongs to a racial minority or, otherwise, a protected class; (2) he or she applied and was qualified for a job for which the employer was seeking applicants; (3) despite the plaintiff's qualifications, he or she was rejected; and (4) after this rejection, the position remained open and the employer continued to seek applicants from persons with the same qualifications as the plaintiff.[26] Other overt discriminatory behavior may also satisfy the requirement. If employers, such as Duke Power Company during the pre-act period, customarily refuse to hire or promote a racial group for certain positions without legitimate business reasons, they may be engaged in intentional discrimination within the meaning of disparate treatment.

In the second step, in which the employer must articulate some legitimate and nondiscriminatory reasons for the employment practice, the employer's burden is not one of persuasion but the production of admissible evidence explaining reasons for the particular practice that is under challenge.[27] Whereas the quantum of evidence required for persuasion is a preponderance of the evidence, the production of evidence is a lesser level of evidence, focusing on a business necessity that a court would accept as legitimate under Title VII. This does not mean that the employer could meet the burden simply by relying on a convenience of business. The employer's explanation of business necessity must be "clear and reasonably specific."[28] What is not required under the burden of production, according to the Court, is for the employer to persuade the trier of fact with "convincing, objective reasons" for selecting one above the other.[29] Having outlined the inner parameters of the employer's defense, the Court added that "although the defendant does not bear a formal burden of persuasion, the defendant nevertheless retains an incentive to persuade the trier of fact that the employment decision was lawful . . . and normally will attempt to prove the factual basis for its explanation."[30]

Clearly then, the burden allocated to the plaintiff is heavier than that allocated to the employer. Why? The Court explains that if the employer, instead of the complainant, was required to persuade by a preponderance of the evidence, employers would more likely than not hire the minority or female applicant whenever that person's objective qualifications were equal to those of a white or a white male applicant.[31] According to Justice Powell, who delivered the opinion for a unanimous Court in *Burdine*, Title VII does not obligate an employer to accord this preference, but allows the employer to choose among equally qualified candidates, provided that the decision is not based upon unlawful criteria.[32]

The third step in the process requires that the plaintiff prove by a preponderance of the evidence that the legitimate reasons offered by the employer were not the true reasons but a pretext or a cover-up for discrimination. The key phrase here, again, is the preponderance of the evidence—the evidence that will persuade the trier of fact that the employer intentionally discriminated against the plaintiff. In this case, the plaintiff may either persuade the court that a discriminatory reason motivated the employer or show that the employer's proffered explanation is unworthy of credence. Also useful for this argument are the specific episodes of the employer's unfair treatment at work or the employer's general policy of minority employment as evidenced by a statistical disparity.[33]

### Disparate Impact Theory

While the disparate impact theory follows the same three-step procedure as in disparate treatment, the required evidentiary standards are more complex and remain controversial. This is because the disparate impact theory focuses on the inference of discrimination on the basis of the consequences of employment practices. The *Griggs* Court determined that a major thrust of Title VII is the consequences of a facially neutral employment policy or practice that may appear fair in form but discriminatory in effect. As in disparate treatment, the Title VII claimant must meet the initial burden of constructing a prima facie case of discrimination. In this case, the plaintiff, according to *Griggs*, does not necessarily have to prove the discriminatory intent of the employer's selection method but need only demonstate that the employer's policies and practices in question created significant adverse impact on a protected group (racial minorities or females). The evidence for this adverse effect usually focuses on statistical disparities.

As a threshold matter, in 1978, the Equal Employment Opportunity Commission, jointly with the Departments of Labor and Justice and the Civil Service Commission, issued the *Uniform Federal Guidelines on Employee Selection Procedures*, suggesting as a rule of thumb at least an 80 percent selection rate for a protected group.[34] Where the applicant pool consists of whites and minority applicants, the 80 percent rule suggests that the selection rate for minority applicants be at least 80 percent that of whites. If, for example, 50 percent of white applicants have been selected, at least 40 percent of minority applicants (80 percent of 50 percent) should have been selected for employment. A statistical disparity is said to exist when the employer's selection method fails to reach this 80 percent threshold, at which point one may be able to construct a prima facie case of discrimination. This method also applies to promotion decisions.[35] The *Uniform Guidelines*, altlernatively, allow concerned persons to look at the composition of an agency's workforce in relation to the surrounding community. An inference of possible discrimination may be drawn if a minority group representation in the employer's workforce is below 80 percent that of whites, in proportion to the surrounding market of relevant labor categories. Statistical comparisons in this case are between the racial composition of the jobs at issue and the racial composition of the qualified population in the relevant job market.[36] The courts are not limited to the 80 percent rule, however. In *Bazemore v. Friday*, the Supreme Court accepted a "strong" multiple regression coefficient as sufficient evidence to make out a prima facie case of discrimination.[37]

Once the plaintiff makes out a prima facie case of discrimination, under the disparate impact theory, the employer must show that the selection procedure is "job-related."[38] According to the *Uniform Guidelines*, the job-relatedness can be demonstrated in several ways, including criterion-related validity, content validity, and construct validity. Whereas criterion-related validity establishes a statistical relationship between job-specific test scores and actual on-the-job performance, content validity measures the congruence between the content of the job and the test instrument. Construct validity examines the actual performance data against the test scores of the applicants, measuring the ability or attributes considered essential although not particularly job-specific.[39] Alternatively, the employer may justify its selection method on the ground of other business necessity, including safety factors (e.g., in the case of substance abusers).

If the employer successfully meets this evidentiary burden, it becomes the task of the plaintiff to persuade the court that "other tests or selection devices, without a similarly undesirable racial effect, would also serve the employer's legitimate interest in efficient and trustworthy workman-ship."[40] This demonstration would be an indication that the employer was using its tests as a cover-up for discrimination.

## Disparate Impact Theory Under Challenge

Recently, the nature of evidentiary standards for the disparate impact approach has shifted significantly, making it more difficult for Title VII claimants to prevail in litigation. Apparently believing that the employer's burden in disparate impact litigation is too onerous, the Court has attempted to reallocate the burden of proof in favor of employers.[41] Disparate impact litigation has generally focused on a professionally developed ability test, and subjected it to empirical validation. But as the Court recognized in *Watson v. Fort Worth Bank & Trust* (1987), employers often rely on subjective criteria for personnel selection and promotion (including common sense, good judgment, originality, ambition, loyalty, and tact), and such subjectve assessments are not easily amenable to scientific validation. Notwithstanding, if employers were required to validate these subjective criteria—which they find difficult, if not impossible—their recourse would be to adopt "surreptitious quota systems" for fear that Title VII complainants might establish a statistical prima facie case.[42] Justice O'Connor, who delivered the plurality opinion in *Watson*, reasoned, "Allowing the evolution of disparate impact analysis to lead to this result would be contrary to Congress' clearly expressed intent [of Title VII]."[43] As safeguards, therefore, the Court suggested that the plaintiff's burden in establishing a prima facie case should go beyond showing the existence of statistical disparities in the employer's work force. The plaintiff must, first, identify the specific employment practice that is considered unlawful and, second, offer "statistical evidence of a kind and degree sufficient to show that the practice in question has caused the exclusion of applicants for jobs or promotions because of their membership in a protected group."[44] The Court also reduced the burden of employers by not requiring them to present formal validation studies. Under the previous model, employers were required to demonstrate that the selection criteria had a manifest relationship to job performance. In *Watson*, the Court did not require employers to introduce formal validation studies even when defending their standardized or objective tests.[45]

In 1989, in *Wards Cove Company v. Antonio*, the Court, in a five to four decision, applied the *Watson* rule in reaching its decision. In this case, nonwhite unskilled cannery workers on the cannery lines at Wards Cove, Alaska, brought a Title VII action against the company under the disparate impact theory, complaining that the company's various hiring and promotion practices had denied them equal opportunity in the allocation of skilled jobs. According to the canery workers, the company's workforce was stratified on racial lines, with unskilled jobs on the cannery lines filled predominantly by nonwhites and skilled jobs on the noncannery lines filled predominantly by whites. The skilled jobs also were paid more—and provided with separate dormitory and mess hall facilities superior to those of the cannery workers. The U.S. District Court for the Western District of Washington and the Ninth Circuit Court of Appeals concluded that the cannery workers made out a prima facie case of disparate impact on the ground of a statistical disparity.

The Supreme Court disagreed with the lower court holdings, invoking the modified disparate impact theory set forth previously in *Watson*. The Court did not think that the evidence of racial stratification constituted a prima facie discrimination, and it pointed out that the statistical comparison between cannery workers and noncannery workers was improper. Relying on *Hazelwood School District v. United States* (1977), the Court maintained that the proper comparison is between the racial composition of the jobs at issue and the racial composition of the qualified population in the relevant labor market. It would make no sense, argued the Court, to compare the number of nonwhites in skilled positions against those in unskilled positions, when in fact the absence of minorities holding such skilled positions is due to a dearth of qualified nonwhite applicants. Even if the statistical comparisons were done properly, they still could not make a prima facie showing of disparate impact on the statistical ground alone.

Relying on *Watson*, the Court, per Justice White, stressed that to establish a prima facie case of discrimination, plaintiffs must go beyond the demonstration of statistical disparities and isolate the specific employment practices responsible for the observed statistical disparities. This would require that the cannery workers demonstrate the statistical disparity to be the "result of one or more of the employment practices . . . specifically showing that each challenged practice has created a significant disparate impact on employment opportunities for whites and nonwhites."[46] According to the *Wards Cove* Court, the cannery workers failed to do so; what they had done was merely allege that several objective employment practices, combined with subjective decision making, resulted in a disparate impact on nonwhites.

Once the prima facie case has been established, the burden shifts to the employer to articulate the reasons for such practice. But the Court suggested that the employer's burden is not to persuade the trier of fact that the challenged practice is essential or indispensable to the employer's business but merely to produce evidence indicating that the "challenged practice serves, in a significant way, the legitimate employment goals of the employer."[47] This is an application of the *Watson* rule requiring a lesser showing than the previous requirement of business necessity or validation studies. When the case reaches this point, the plaintiff ultimately must prove that discrimination has been caused by a specific employment practice. Alternatively, the plaintiff must persuade the trier of fact that other tests or selection devices, without a similarly undesirable racial effect, would also serve the employer's legitimate hiring interests. Again, relying on *Watson*, the Court added that "the cost or other burdens of proposed alternative selection devices are relevant in determining whether they would be equally as effective as the challenged practice in serving the employer's legitimate business goals."[48] Acknowledging that the courts are less competent than employers to restructure business practices, the Court cautioned that "the judiciary . . . proceed with care before mandating that an employer must adopt a plaintiff's alternative selection or hiring practice in response to a Title VII suit."

*Watson* and *Wards Cove* make it clear that the Court is embarking on a new direction in disparate impact litigation. No longer does the Court deem a statistical disparity alone sufficient to raise the first impression of discrimination. Title VII claimants now must additionally demonstrate the causal connection between statistical disparities and specific employment practices. As Justice Stevens contended in *Wards Cove*, this is clearly a retreat from the view expressed in *Griggs v. Duke Power*. In *Griggs*, the Court was concerned about practices that are fair in form but discriminatory in effect, thereby focusing on the consequences of such practices. In *Watson* and *Wards Cove*, the Court exhibited concern not only with the consequences, but also with the specific employment practices responsible for a particular statistical disparity. This new requirement—whether it is empirically feasible or not—brings the disparate impact approach closer to the disparate treatment approach.[49] Another important departure is the employer's explanation of business necessity. *Griggs* and the *Uniform Guidelines* required the employer, when challenged, to meet the burden of showing that the selection procedure is job-related, as evidenced by validation studies. In *Watson* and *Wards Cove*, the Court relaxed the employer's burden significantly by no longer requiring formal validation studies that would show that particular criteria predict actual on-the-job performance. These developments, no doubt, add uncertainties to the concept of disparate impact within the meaning of Title VII.

## EMPLOYER LIABILITY

Suppose that Title VII claimants ultimately prevail. What remedies are available? Title VII (Section 703(g)) provides that the court "may order such affirmative action as may be appropriate, which may include, but not limited to, reinstatement or hiring of employees, with or without backpay . . . or any other equitable relief as the court deems appropriate." On first glance, it appears that the statute places Title VII remedies entirely within the district court's discretion. This is not entirely correct. In *Albermarle Paper Company v. Moody* (1975), the Supreme Court required that the district court's back pay decision be measured against the purpose of Title VII, which is "to make persons whole for injuries suffered on account of unlawful employment discrimination."[50] The Court reasoned:

> If employers were faced only with the prospect of an injunctive order, they would have little incentive to shun practices of dubious legality.

It is the reasonably certain prospect of a backpay award that provides the spur or catalyst which causes employers and unions to self-examine and to self-evaluate their employment practices and to endeavor to eliminate, so far as possible, the last vestiges of an unfortunate and ignominious page in this country's history.[51]

The make-whole principle is a legal remedy that requires an injured party to be placed "as near as may be possible in the situation he or she would have occupied if the wrong had not been committed."[52] For Title VII, this means the awarding of back pay and retroactive seniority. How far may this award go back? As was determined in *Albermarle Paper Company v. Moody*, back pay and retroactive seniority cannot be awarded further back than the date of Title VII—1972 for the public sector and 1964 for the private sector. Should the make-whole remedy be extended to the unnamed parties in a lawsuit as well? The *Albermale* Court believed that back pay under Title VII should be awarded on a class basis so that unnamed class members would not need to exhaust administrative procedures.[53] In this connection, the Court explained that the make-whole principle is designed to compensate workers for their injuries, not to punish employers. Thus, good intent or bad faith is immaterial—since the thrust of Title VII is directed to the consequences of employment practices, not simply the motivation. The absence of bad faith does not redeem the employer from the obligation to make whole.[54]

One final note concerning attorney fees: In civil lawsuits, plaintiffs' attorney fees may become prohibitively high depending on the complexity of litigation, and they often serve as a deterrent to litigation. In 1976, Congress enacted the Civil Rights Attorneys' Fees Award Act, incorporating it as part of the Civil Rights Statute as codifed at 42 U.S.C. 2000(e). Under this act, which was adopted with an aim to enforce the Civil Rights Statute, the successful Title VII claimant may recover attorney fees from the employer.[55]

## SUMMARY AND CONCLUSION

In this chapter we have briefly examined the evolution of the Equal Protection Clause as it relates to equal employment opportunity. In public policy and administration, technical standards are often just as critical as the purpose of legislation, because weak and misconceived enforcement standards can make the law almost meaningless. Thus, we have looked at the enforcement aspect of Title VII—the Equal Employment Opportunity Act of 1964 as amended in 1972—and have briefly reviewed several

Supreme Court cases that identify what employment practices are considered unlawful discrimination, what evidence is needed to prove (or defend) the charges, and what the scope of the employer's liability may be when it is found not to be in compliance with EEO requirements.

To summarize the key point, Title VII, as interpreted by the Supreme Court, proscribes not only employment practices that are intentionally discriminatory, but also such practices that are fair in form but discriminatory in consequence. As a matter of long-standing practice, therefore, the Court has required that, to show disparate treatment, Title VII claimants must construct a prima facie case of discrimination by a preponderance of the evidence—that the employer's policy or practice is intended to discriminate against a protected group. For disparate impact, Title VII claimants must establish a prima facie case of discrimination on the basis of employment consequences as evidenced by a statistical disparity.

Once the plaintiff has been successful in raising the first impression of discrimination, the employer has an opportunity to rebut the charges for the reason of a business necessity—a legitimate excuse Title VII recognizes. Here, the disparate treatment approach looks for specific and clear business reasons, but the disparate impact approach usually focuses on validation studies. Under the circumstances, however, the Court generally respects the employer's judgment. In *New York City Transit Authority v. Beazer* (1978), the Court accepted the Transit Authority's explanation as legitimate when, for safety reasons, it excluded from safety-sensitive subway operations persons receiving methadone maintenance treatment to cure heroin addiction.[56] In the final step in the process, Title VII claimants in both cases must persuade the court that the employer's explanation is a pretext unworthy of credence.

During the past few years, the Court has been moving to reallocate the evidentiary burdens for disparate impact. The Court now requires Title VII claimants relying on disparate impact to prove a causal connection between specific employment practices and particular statistical disparities, thereby making it more difficult for Title VII claimants to construct a prima facie case of discrimination. With respect to the employer's burden, the Court also tends to relax the long-standing requirement of validation studies. The Court requires employers, under the disparate impact challenge, to show that the challenged practices serve in a significant way their legitimate business goals. Under this rule, no longer are employers required to show that the challenged practice is "essential or indispensable" to their business. These changes create a great deal of uncertainty in equal employment opportunity litigation under Title VII.[57] Blacks, other racial minorities, and women have come a long way in their struggle for equal employment opportunity. The battle is still not over, and much remains to be seen.

## NOTES

1. *Bazemore v. Friday*, 106 S. Ct. 3000, 3006–3007 (1986).
2. *The Independent Weekly*, October 9, 1989, 11.
3. Ibid., 12.
4. *Plessy v. Ferguson*, 163 U.S. 537 (1896).
5. Yong S. Lee, "Civil Liability of State and Local Government," *Public Administration Review* 47, no. 2 (March/April 1987), 160–170.
6. *Brown v. Board of Education*, 347 U.S. 483 (1954).
7. *Plessy*, 543.
8. Ibid., 544.
9. Ibid., 557.
10. Ibid., 559.
11. *Brown*, 493.
12. Ibid., 495.
13. Ibid., 492.
14. Ibid., 494.
15. Thomas R. Dye, *Understanding Public Policy* (Englewood Cliffs, N.J.: Prentice Hall, 1978), 43–74.
16. *Patterson v. McLean Credit Union*, 491 U.S. 164 (1989).
17. The Civil Rights Act of 1964, Title VII, Section 703(a).
18. Ibid., Section 703(h).
19. *Griggs v. Duke Power*, 401 U.S. 424, 431 (1970).
20. Ibid., 436.
21. Ibid., 429–430.
22. Ibid., 430.
23. Ibid., 432.
24. 411 U.S. 792 (1973).
25. 450 U.S. 248 (1981).
26. *McDonnell Douglas Corp. v. Green*, 411 U.S. 792, 802 (1972).
27. *Texas Department of Community Affairs v. Burdine*, 450 U.S. 248, 256 (1981).
28. Ibid., 258.
29. Ibid.
30. Ibid.
31. Ibid., 259.
32. Ibid.
33. *McDonnell Douglas*, 805.
34. *The Uniform Guidelines on Employee Selection Procedures, Federal Register*, vol. 43, no. 166, (August 25, 1978).
35. *Watson v. Fort Worth Bank & Trust*, 487 U.S. 977 (1987).
36. *Hazelwood School District v. United States*, 433 U.S. 299, 308 (1977).
37. Yong S. Lee, "Shaping Judicial Response to Gender Discrimination in Employment Compensation," *Public Administration Review* 49, no. 5 (September/October 1989), 420–430.

38. *Griggs*, 425. See also *Albemarle Paper Company v. Moody*, 422 U.S. 405, 425 (1975).

39. For further reference, see *The Uniform Guidelines*.

40. *Albermarle*, 425.

41. See *Watson*.

42. Ibid., 991–992.

43. Ibid., 994.

44. Ibid.

45. Ibid., 998.

46. *Wards Cove Company v. Antonio*, 57 LW 4583, 4587 (June 6, 1989).

47. Ibid., 4588.

48. Ibid.

49. A study of specific causal connections may require an unbundling of the decision process. The unbundling may or may not be possible depending on the sophistication and formalization of the decision process. Assuming that unbundling is possible, a causal analysis may become difficult, if not impossible, when a particular statistical disparity occurs not so much from a particular policy or practice but from the interaction of several policies and the behavior of the employer acting even in good faith.

50. *Albermarle*, 418.

51. Ibid., 417–418.

52. Jay M. Shafritz, Albert C.Hyde, and David H. Rosenbloom, *Personnel Management in Government*, 3rd ed., (New York and Basel: Marcel Dekker, 1986), 200.

53. *Albermarle*, see footnote 8.

54. Ibid., 422.

55. *Maine v. Thiboutot*, 448 U.S. 1 (1980).

56. 440 U.S. 568 (1978).

57. Disenchanted with the new direction the Court has been taking in Title VII litigation, in 1990 Congress passed a new civil rights bill to undo much of what the Supreme Court has done under the *Watson* rule. But the bill did not survive a presidential veto. A modified version of the bill is being debated at the time of this writing in Congress.

# 5

# Affirmative Action and the Constitution

In a plurality opinion, the U.S. Supreme Court in *University of California Regents v. Bakke* (1978) was able to establish one important constitutional principle—that a carefully and properly designed affirmative action program would not be constitutionally impermissible.[1] Since *Bakke*, the Court has handed down several decisions on affirmative action, articulating in greater detail how to evaluate affirmative action policies and programs. What has emerged from these efforts is a so-called two-tier analysis. The framework, which was first outlined in *Bakke*, expanded in Justice Powell's concurring opinion in *Fullilove v. Klutznick* (1980),[2] and applied in *Wygant v. Jackson Board of Education* (1985),[3] establishes that the validity of affirmative action plans is to be determined on two sets of principles: "a compelling governmental interest" and "narrowly tailored means." These principles will be discussed shortly.

Some have argued that the Supreme Court has reached a workable consensus with respect to how to deal with affirmative action policy.[4] This chapter argues that this observation is correct only in the most general sense.[5] An examination of Court decisions during the last decade reveals that the level of scrutiny the Court has applied under the two-tier framework is far from consistent. As a matter of fact, the Court has been vacillating with a great latitude over what qualifies as a compelling interest and also how precisely or narrowly a remedy should be tailored. In November 1989 in *City of Richmond v. Croson Co.*, the divided Court for the first time applied the strict scrutiny standard;[6] but six months later in *Metro Broadcasting Inc. v. Federal Communications Commission*, the

same Court, again in a narrow majority, reverted to its previous intermediate standard.[7]

This chapter considers several questions: Why has the Court not been
able to agree on a review standard? What factors in the two-tier framework
make judicial review so onerous? What can public administrators expect
from the future Court? This chapter attempts to provide a perspective on
these questions. First, it describes the analytical framework the Court
employs in reviewing affirmative action cases. Second, it evaluates the
various ways this framework has been applied in the past. Third, it explores
the different and often conflicting views that individual Supreme Court
justices have taken with respect to affirmative action vis-à-vis the Equal
Protection Clause. Here, attention is focused on three justices—Powell,
Brennan, and O'Connor—all of whom have led the Court in significant
affirmative action decisions. The analysis presented suggests that the
two-tier framework for affirmative action that is being employed is not a
systematic test enabling coherent application across related cases, but
rather represents a set of largely conflicting and often polarized value
preferences. This conglomerate framework—perhaps a response to a
"constitutional stalemate"[8]—has permitted the making of essentially inconsistent choices, depending on which justice and whose values ultimately
forge the Court opinion at a particular time. This explains, at least in part,
why the level of scrutiny applied to affirmative action in the past has
differed from case to case.

## JUDICIAL AMBIVALENCE

In *City of Richmond v. Croson Co.* the Court divided five to four in
rejecting Richmond's 30 percent set-aside program (Minority Business
Utilization). The city argued that blacks, among others, should be viewed
as being the victims of society-wide discrimination who have been manifestly underrepresented in the city's construction industry. The Court's
majority did not agree, however, that rectifying the manifest imbalance
amounted to a compelling governmental interest. In *Metro Broadcasting
Inc. v. Federal Communications Commission*, the Court went back to the
application of its previous intermediate scrutiny standard and upheld the
FCC's preferential broadcast licensing program. The FCC used the same
argument that Richmond had used earlier—that blacks, as victims of
society-wide discrimination, were underrepresented in the nation's broadcasting industry. While the two cases are somewhat different in that *Croson*
dealt with a local government action and *Metro Broadcasting* a federal
action, a careful reading of Justice O'Connor's dissenting view in *Metro*

*Broadcasting* dispels any speculation that the difference was due to the federal-local difference. O'Connor would have the Court apply to *Metro Broadcasting* the same strict scrutiny standard she had earlier applied in *Croson*. To O'Connor, the narrow majority in *Metro Broadcasting* unwisely relied on "an intermediate standard of review" that is "too amorphous, too unsubstantial, and too unrelated to any legitimate basis for employing racial classification."[9]

An analysis of the Supreme Court's affirmative action decisions, including dissenting views, during the last decade shows that the Court has often acknowledged the inconsistency in application of the two-prong test framework. Justice Brennan addressed this issue directly when he wrote in *Sheet Metal Workers v. EEOC* (1986): "We have consistently recognized that government bodies constitutionally may adopt racial classifications as a remedy for past discrimination, [but] we have not agreed . . . on the proper test to be applied in analyzing the constitutionality of race-conscious remedial measures."[10] Justice O'Connor's dissenting opinion in *U.S. v. Paradise* (1987) also reflected this concern.[11] When *Paradise* upheld Alabama's race-based promotion quota, O'Connor criticized the Court for having adopted "a standardless view of 'narrowly tailored' far less stringent than that required by strict scrutiny."[12] While *Johnson v. Transportation Agency* (1987) is not a constitutional case, it still provides another example of the Court's shifting ground. The *Johnson* Court accepted Santa Clara County's manifest imbalance argument as fit grounds for its gender-based promotion decision. Note that the manifest imbalance argument earlier had been used in *United Steelworkers v. Weber* in 1979— a private sector affirmative action case.[13] But in *Johnson*, Justice Scalia was critical of the Court majority for having applied a private-sector rule to a public sector affirmative action decision. In his view, the Court should have applied the prior discrimination standard set forth in *Wygant*, a public employment case. If the Court had taken that route, the *Johnson* case would have been decided in an entirely different way.[14]

Similarly, in *Croson* the Court held that while Congress may have the authority to address the problem of societal discrimination, a state or a local governmental body may not. While agreeing with the Court, Justice Scalia went further to insist that "strict scrutiny [must] be applied to all government classification by race"—presumably meaning both federal and local—"whether or not its asserted purpose is 'remedial' or 'benign.' "[15] Justice Marshall protested vigorously, arguing that "[a] profound difference separates governmental actions that themselves are racist, and governmental actions that seek to remedy the effects of prior racism or to prevent neutral governmental activity from perpetuating the effects of such racism."[16] The soon-to-be retiring justice insisted, in dissent, that "remedial programs should not be subjected to conventional 'strict scrutiny'—scrutiny that is strict in theory, but fatal in fact."[17]

The point of these sampled views is to underscore the strain that goes on in the Court searching for consensus as to the judicial review framework appropriate for affirmative action policy disputes.[18] This strain and attendant ambiguity leave affirmative action in a continuing state of uncertainty.[19] Perhaps, as many in Congress believe, affirmative action requires clearer legislative guidance. But as evidenced by the failed 1990 civil rights bill, the political system also seems to have reached an impasse, at least temporarily.[20] This leaves public administrators trapped in the middle, in a sense, and they are expected to act as best as they can but without clear direction. A recent controversy created by the U.S. Department of Education (DOE) over black scholarships exemplifies the point. On December 12, 1990 an assistant secretary of education wrote to Fiesta Bowl organizers in Arizona objecting to their attempt to establish black scholarship funds.[21] Relying on the strict scrutiny standard applied in *Croson*, the assistant secretary declared that a black scholarship fund would be tantamount to a racial classification in violation of the Equal Protection Clause of the Fourteenth Amendment. He wrote that schools awarding such scholarships would risk losing federal funds. This declaration of opinion raised considerable public uproar and anguish among minority students on college campuses, and the White House reluctantly intervened, persuading the DOE to stay the declaration temporarily.[22] The DOE complied,[23] but it wanted to go on record to say that such scholarships are illegal while acknowledging that the situation will not be clarified until there is a court decision.[24]

## CASES FOR ANALYSIS

The observations presented here are based upon an analysis of nine affirmative action decisions delivered by the U.S. Supreme Court over the course of the last decade. The cases are listed in Table 5.1 below. The analysis begins with *University of California Regents v. Bakke* (1978) because it marked a turning point in the constitutional history of affirmative action. The point made by Justice Powell with four other justices (Brennan, Marshall, White, and Blackmun) joining in the majority opinion, was that a carefully designated affirmative action program would be constitutionally permissible.[25] While each case in Table 5.1 presents unique factual circumstances, the purpose here is to understand the degree to which an identifiable judicial standard of review has devel-

**Table 5.1**
**Major Affirmative Action Decisions Delivered by the U.S. Supreme Court from 1978 to 1990**

| Supreme Court Case | Year | Employer | Affirmative Action at Issue |
|---|---|---|---|
| UC Regents v. Bakke | 1978 | Univ. of Calif. (Davis Campus) | A fixed admission quota to the medical school |
| Fullilove v. Klutznick | 1980 | Economic Dev. Adm (Federal gov't) | A 10% MBE* set-aside in public works projects. |
| Wygant v. Jackson Bd of Education | 1985 | Jackson School Bd. | Layoffs in violation of seniority |
| Sheet Metal Workers v. EEOC | 1986 | Local 28, Sheet Metal Union | A 29% nonwhite membership quota under consent decree |
| Firefighters v. City of Cleveland | 1986 | City of Cleveland | A fixed number of promotions reserved for minorities who were nonvictims |
| U.S. v. Paradise | 1987 | State Public Safety Department | A temporary 50% promotional quota under consent decree |
| Johnson v. Transportation Agency | 1987 | Santa Clara County | A preferential promotion of woman over man |
| City of Richmond v. J.A. Croson | 1989 | City of Richmond | A 30% of MBE set-aside in city construction contracts |
| Metro Broadcasting Inc. v. FCC | 1990 | Federal Communications Commission | Preferential awarding in comparative licensing proceedings |

*MBE represents Minority Business Enterprises.

oped over time. To gain insights into the interaction of different values in the judicial process, attention is paid to all opinions filed, including concurring and dissenting views. In an effort to focus more sharply on the "level of scrutiny" debate, we look at affirmative action decisions exclusively, leaving aside the numerous antidiscrimination cases that might be related in equal opportunity adjudication. While antidiscrimination decisions are generally relevant to the discussion of equal protection, such cases are different from affirmative action cases, and require a separate analysis.

## JUDICIAL STANDARDS OF REVIEW

*University of California Regents v. Bakke* (1978) was a complex legal challenge, and the Court was unable to produce a majority opinion. Even so, the *Bakke* Court set forth an important constitutional principle, that under the Equal Protection Clause "[r]acial and ethnic distinctions of any sort are inherently suspect and thus call for the most exact judicial examination."[26] Since the rights established by the Fourteenth Amendment are "personal rights," it was established that when government takes an action that "touche[s] upon an individual's race or ethnic background, [the individual] is entitled to a judicial determination that the burden he is asked to bear on that basis is *precisely tailored* to serve a *compelling governmental interest* (emphasis added)."[27] *Bakke*, however, did not elaborate on exactly how to determine what government interests qualify as "compelling interests," and what types of remedies may satisfy the requirement for precisely-tailored means. Much of the Court debate in the post-*Bakke* era has centered on the elaboration of this two-tier framework.

### What Constitutes a Compelling Interest

If a race-conscious remedy must be preconditioned by a compelling state interest, what circumstances may support a determination that a state interest is, indeed, compelling? At least four competing justifications have entered the debate: societal (historical) discrimination, a manifest racial (or gender) imbalance, prior discrimination, and blanket prohibitions.[28] The societal discrimination theory, which represents a liberal view, asserts that race-conscious remedies are permissible if such remedies are designed to serve the important governmental objectives of eradicating societal discrimination.[29] The theory does not require a showing of prior discrimination by the agency involved or a particular statistical disparity in the racial composition of the agency's workforce as related to the relevant labor market. It merely relies on the historical discrimination practiced at the societal level.[30]

In *Fullilove v. Klutznick* (1980) and again ten years later in *Metro Broadcasting Inc. v. Federal Communications Commission* (1990), both of which involved federal action, the Court accepted the social discrimination argument as a valid ground to satisfy the compelling interest requirement. At issue in *Fullilove* was a federal statute establishing an MBE (Minority Business Enterprise) set-aside quota as a means of eradicating societal discrimination. Metro Broadcasting involved FCC policies awarding preferences for minority ownership in comparative proceedings for new licenses.

The other extreme is what Justice Stevens labelled the "blanket prohibition" theory in *Johnson v. Transportation Agency* (1987). This theory maintains that the Equal Protection Clause applies to every citizen, majority or minority, in a color-blind fashion and permits no discriminatory preference, whether the remedial action involves quota hiring, quota promotion, or preferential protection of minorities and women against layoffs.[31] In Justice Stewart's words, "[t]he equal protection standard of the Constitution has one clear and central meaning—it absolutely prohibits invidious discrimination by government" (*Fullilove v. Klutznick*, p. 2796).

The manifest imbalance theory, which was recognized in *United Steelworkers v. Weber* (1980) and in *Johnson v. Transportation Agency* (1987), holds that remedying a manifest racial (or gender) imbalance in traditionally segregated job categories is a compelling interest sufficient to permit a governmental agency or a private employer to adopt a limited race-conscious remedy (*United Steelworkers v. Weber*, p. 2724; *Johnson v. Transportation Agency*, p. 1452). The manifest imbalance is measured by a statistical disparity in the racial or gender composition of an employer's workforce, internally and externally, to its relevant labor market.

The prior discrimination theory presumes the existence of a compelling interest when the agency involved demonstrates the specific instances of illegal discrimination in its past. The circumstance is considered compelling in a sense that the agency now plans to address the past wrongs of its own making.[32] In *Wygant v. Jackson Board of Education* (1985), the Court emphatically required that race-conscious remedies be justified by a compelling state interest, and that a compelling state interest, in turn, be justified by "some showing of prior discrimination by the governmental unit involved" (*Wygant v. Jackson Board of Education*, p. 274). In *City of Richmond v. Croson Co.* (1989), the Court rejected Richmond's affirmative action plan because it failed, among other things, to show prior discrimination.

### The Principle of Narrowly-Tailored Means

A compelling interest is a necessary but not a sufficient condition for providing a race-conscious remedy. The other condition is the requirement for a "narrowly-tailored means." This means that the chosen remedies must be closely fit to the purpose they seek to advance. In his concurring opinion in *Fullilove*, Justice Powell suggested that the remedies under question be examined in terms of (1) the efficacy of other race-neutral alternatives, (2) the duration of the remedies, (3) the population base for comparison, (4) their flexibility, and (5) their effects on innocent third parties. The criteria have been variously applied in later affirmative action cases, but no general consensus has as yet emerged with respect to their precise application.[33] The criteria of third-party effects and consideration of other race-neutral means have been most contentious in the affirmative action debate.

The concept of duration looks at whether a chosen remedy has been instituted temporarily or indefinitely. The Court has been adamantly opposed to affirmative action plans that are designed to maintain a racial (or gender) balance, which implies permanence.[34] With regard to flexibility, the Court looks at whether or not the plan would waive the affirmative action requirement when it becomes practically unattainable. Both the duration and flexibility standards are technical requirements and have not caused much controversy.

For population comparison the Court requires that the employer analyze the racial (and/or gender) composition of its internal workforce and also compare it with the relevant labor market. The relevant labor market may involve a local geographical boundary, or that part of the workforce that is functionally relevant for comparison. As different professions require different functional boundaries, the Court at times has had a difficult methodological problem. In *United Steelworkers*, *Paradise*, and *Johnson*, for instance, the Court had no difficulty in accepting a workforce analysis that compared the racial (and gender) composition of the internal work force in relation to its local labor market; but in *Wygant* and *Croson* the Court had difficulty accepting the methodologies employed by the respective employers. In *Wygant* the Jackson School Board compared the percentage of minority teachers to that of minority students, under the "role model" theory. The Court rejected the premise, suggesting that "the proper comparison in this case is between the racial composition of the school's teaching staff and that of the qualified public school teachers in the relevant labor market."[35] In *Croson* the Court rejected the city's MBE set-aside plan as invalid, in part because Richmond failed to show "a significant statistical disparity between the number of qualified minority contractors willing and able to perform a particular service and the number of such contractors actually engaged by the locality or the locality's prime contractors."[36]

The effects on innocent third parties (or the issue of reverse discrimination) involve individual rights guaranteed by the Equal Protection Clause. Leading the Court in *Wygant*, Justice Powell set forth the basic parameters for analyzing third party effects. "As part of this Nation's dedication to eradicating racial discrimination," Powell wrote, "innocent persons may be called upon to bear some of the burden of the remedy to cure the effects of prior discrimination and such a sharing of the burden by innocent parties is not impermissible. . . . Yet this burden should not be too intrusive."[37] By intrusiveness Powell meant the relative weight of injury sustained by the innocent third parties—for instance, between the direct personal burden that laid-off teachers at Jackson public schools had to suffer and the type of burden that the association of construction contractors in *Fullilove* had to shoulder in 1980 when the association only had limited access to public works funds. Powell thought that the impact of the 10 percent federal works funds set-aside for minority-owned business firms was "relatively light" compared to the burden created by layoffs.[38] He also revisited *DeFunis v. Odegaard* (1974)[39] to note that when DeFunis was denied admission to the University of Washington Law School because of the university's affirmative action plan, his burden was not heavy because he already had been accepted by several other law schools.[40] The *Wygant* Court laid down a general rule that a third-party burden associated with hiring goals may be constitutionally permissible because it is defused considerably among society generally and forecloses only one of several opportunities. The burden, however, may be considered too intrusive and thus constitutionally impermissible if and when the plan takes away another person's job, threatens the job security, or even temporarily disrupts his or her life via layoffs.[41]

In *Bakke* Justice Powell did not apply this line of reasoning. It was Justice Brennan in *Sheet Metal Workers v. EEOC* (1986) who employed it successfully, arguing that the temporary union membership quota under a consent decree was not necessarily trammeling.[42] Promotion decisions were the central issues in *Firefighters v. City of Cleveland* (1986),[43] *U.S. v. Paradise* (1987), and *Johnson v. Transportation Agency* (1987). Employers in each of these cases used either a limited quota or a preferential consideration system, and the Court did not believe that the third party effects in these cases were impermissibly intrusive. Preferential awarding of contracts and licenses represented the controversy in *Fullilove v. Klutznick* (1980) and *Metro Broadcasting Inc. v. Federal Communications Commission* (1990) to which the Court applied the same rationale as in admissions and membership. In *Firefighters v. Stotts* (1984),[44] the Court dealt with the reverse bumping of senior members in favor of junior black employees. In this case, the Court concluded that the action was constitutionally impermissible.

Perhaps the most controversial part of the narrowly tailored means requirement is the efficacy test, that is, the consideration of other race-neutral alternatives before resorting to quotas. Efficacy does not necessarily require, according to Justice Powell, "the least restrictive means."[45] What it requires is that public agencies not resort to a racial classification or a quota improperly and without examining other available means. This approach embraces both conceptual and value dilemmas. Conceptually, the difficulty is how comprehensively an agency should identify race-neutral alternatives and how rigorously it should test their effectiveness before resorting to even a temporary quota system. In terms of value conflicts, some would favor a strict scrutiny position, objecting to the use of racial quotas at all, and others would favor a more open, liberal position permitting classification if it were to advance benign public policy objectives. In-between are found two groups: one favoring the use of race or gender only as a "plus" factor in the equation and the other permitting the use of limited quotas, provided that the challenged plan had met all other criteria. In the final analysis, no consensus seems to exist on this efficacy test.

To sum up the discussion so far, there appears to be a general agreement that an affirmative action program should operate as a temporary measure, and with flexibility demonstrated by a waiver provision. But more importantly, the consensus seems to be that affirmative action programs must not produce trammeling effects on innocent third parties. In this connection, the effects of affirmative action plans on admission, membership, hiring, promotion, licensing, and bidding have seldom been found to be trammeling or impermissibly intrusive. Analysis of cases under study shows that the application of these rules has been consistent in Court opinions.

The disagreements in the Court appear to exist primarily in the efficacy test and the justification for a compelling interest. The Court has not reached the consensus on whether, for proper remedial purposes, race and gender may be treated as plus factors or can be classified in a limited way (meaning a limited quota). By definition, the color-blind approach to affirmative action negates the very idea of affirmative action, so it is beyond the scope of this discussion. With respect to the compelling interest criteria, the Court has shown a considerable latitude over its justification—from prior discrimination to manifest imbalance and societal discrimination, depending on which justice on the Court is able to forge the consensus.

Clearly, then, the variation of Court decisions, at least during the past decade, could be traceable to what appears to be the lack of consensus among Court justices over the efficacy test and what may be considered to be a compelling interest for a remedial action. For the purpose of simplicity, these two criteria are placed on a two-dimensional grid in Figure 5.1. The grid should provide a useful framework for examining the considerable variance in the Court's affirmative action decisions since the *Bakke* decision.

The configuration in Figure 5.1 indicates that under existing judicial standards of review the Court is capable of ruling in several ways on any particular case. Also in the configuration is seen a rough continuum from stricter scrutiny to less strict scrutiny—stricter in a sense that it moves towards the rigid application of the color-blind approach of the Equal Protection Clause. When the Court applies standard I, it would permit the employer to use race (or gender) as only a plus factor in employment decisions, provided that it demonstrates a compelling interest on the basis of prior discrimination. Under standard II, the Court would endorse a limited quota only under the condition that the employer demonstrates prior discrimination and that it uses the classification with due consideration of all safeguards. Most important, the plan should not produce trammeling effects. Standard V is less strict than standard I in that the employer is not required to prove prior discrimination but only to show a statistical disparity in the racial or gender composition of its workforce in traditionally segregated job categories. The showing of prior discrimination is a requirement considered much more stringent than that of a statistical disparity required by a manifest imbalance. Standard IX is considered most liberal, in that it allows a benign (not malevolent) racial classification as a means to accomplish important governmental objectives.

**Figure 5.1**
**The Different Levels of Scrutiny Potentially Available under the Two-Tier Analysis**

|  | Remedial Action | | |
| --- | --- | --- | --- |
| Justification for a Compelling Interest | A "Plus" Factor | Limited Quota | Benign Quota |
| Prior Discrimination | I | II | III |
| Manifest Imbalance | IV | V | VI |
| Society-wide Discrimination | VII | VIII | IX |

## THE PATTERNS OF JUDICIAL REVIEW

Figure 5.2 below plots affirmative action cases on the grid depicted in Figure 5.1. The placement of cases is based on the standards of review that the Court used in upholding or rejecting the agency argument. Case names where the Court rejected the agency argument appear in bold-face; in the cases shown in parenthesis the Court opinions discuss how the programs under review might otherwise have been justified. In *Paradise*, the Alabama Public Safety Department used a promotion quota for promotion under a consent decree, and the Court upheld the plan on the grounds that the quota was used in a limited way and that the department provided sufficient evidence of past discrimination. Thus, *Paradise* is considered as a standard II decision. In *Croson*, the Court rejected the city's argument that the manifest imbalance theory justified its set-aside program. Nor did the Court agree with the argument that the benign classification the city used

**Figure 5.2**
**The Different Levels of Scrutiny as Applied to Affirmative Action Cases**

| | Remedial Action | | |
|---|---|---|---|
| Justification for a Compelling Interest | A "Plus" Factor | Limited Quota | Benign Quota |
| Prior Discrimination | *(Croson)* | *(Bakke); Paradise; Sheet Metal Firefighters* | |
| Manifest Imbalance | *Johnson* | **Wygant** | ***Croson*** |
| Society-wide Discrimination | | | ***Bakke Fullilove Metro Broadcasting*** |

The cases in bold were rejected for having used the standards in the grid.

Otherwise, the cases were upheld on the basis of the standards used in the grid.

The cases in parenthesis, according to the Court, should have used the standards in the grid.

would satisfy the requirement of narrowly tailored means. Thus, *Croson* is placed in the standard VI category in bold, indicating that the plan was rejected. We also place *Croson* in standard I within parentheses, because the Court rejected Richmond's plan not only for failure to show prior discrimination but also for failure to have it narrowly tailored. The Court's preferred alternative in this case was a race-neutral means, something akin to a plus consideration.

### Standard I: A Plus Consideration to Remedy Prior Discrimination

The argument advanced by the Court in *City of Richmond v. Croson Co.* comes closest to what standard I would require. Note that the city of Richmond implemented a 30 percent set-aside of its construction contracts for minority business firms. In applying the two-tier analysis, the Court concluded that Richmond failed on almost all accounts. First, as the Court pointed out, Richmond failed to prove prior discrimination. Second, Richmond's plan was not narrowly tailored, especially in the waiver provision and time duration. Third, and most important, the city used a benign quota, which the Court argued was in violation of the Equal Protection Clause. Leading the Court, Justice O'Connor alluded to a possibility that Richmond's plan might have been reviewed favorably if it had used race as a plus factor on a case-by-case approach.[46] It is well to remember that earlier in *Johnson v. Transportation Agency* (1987), O'Connor concurred with the Court because "Joyce's sex was simply used as a 'plus' factor."[47]

### Standard II: A Limited Quota to Remedy Prior Discrimination

Standard II would allow an agency to resort to a limited quota as a means to remedy past illegal discrimination of its own making. This has been the case in the *Bakke, Wygant, Firefighters v. Cleveland, Sheet Metal Workers*, and *Paradise* cases. The *Bakke* decision fits standard II because the split Court invalidated the University of California, Davis admission program not only for failure to show prior discrimination but also for failure to have its admission program narrowly tailored. More specifically, the quota system was arguably used to maintain a racial balance, not for a short duration but more or less permanently and without consideration of other race-neutral alternatives. In *Wygant* the Court rejected the Jackson School Board's decision to layoff tenured nonminority teachers while retaining minority teachers on probationary status because the classification scheme used was neither narrowly tailored nor justified by identifiable prior discrimination. But most important, the school board's decision was considered too intrusive on individual rights guaranteed under the Equal Protection Clause because it caused "trammeling effects" on innocent third parties. In *Sheet Metal Workers* as well as in *Paradise*, the Court endorsed the membership and promotion quotas, respectively, because the allocated quotas under consent decree were deemed narrowly tailored and justified by past illegal discrimination.

### Standard IV: A Plus Consideration to Eliminate a Manifest Imbalance

Standard IV is applied when race or gender has been taken into account as a plus factor in personnel decision making as a means to eliminate a manifest imbalance in traditionally segregated job categories. *Johnson v. Transportation Agency* fits standard IV. Santa Clara County promoted a female employee over a male employee to a road dispatcher position even though the male employee scored slightly higher in the interview score. The Court let Santa Clara's decision stand, on the grounds that women were manifestly underrepresented in traditionally segregated job categories, and that the county voluntarily established the plan with a long-term goal of attaining (not maintaining) a balanced work force. It is not inappropriate, observed the Court, that the county took gender into consideration (i.e., as a plus factor) in a case-by-case approach.[48]

### Standard VI: A Limited Quota to Eliminate a Manifest Imbalance

Medical school administration programs at the University of California, Davis and a minority business set-aside program in the City of Richmond were both formulated using standard VI, which relies on the idea of benign classification under a manifest imbalance. Since the Court rejected both programs, respectively, standard VI, at least at the present time, appears to be a nonviable affirmative action standard. In both cases, however, the Court was narrowly split in its opinion.

### Standard IX: A Benign Classification and Public Policy

Standard IX allows the use of a benign (broad in this case) quota as a means to eradicate the continuing effects of past society-wide discrimination. *Fullilove v. Klutznick* and *Metro Broadcasting Inc. v. Federal Communications Commission*—both federal employer cases—represent the application of standard IX. In *Fullilove*, several associations of construction contractors filed a lawsuit, complaining that the Minority Business Enterprise (MBE) provision of the Public Works Employment Act of 1977 on its face violated the Equal Protection Clause and the Due Process Clause of the Fifth Amendment. The MBE provision required that at least 10 percent of federal grants be used by state and local grantees to procure services from minority groups. The Court, led by Chief Justice Burger, held that Congress under its legislative authority had a right to enact the MBE provision in the remedial context and that "when effectuating a limited and properly tailored remedy to cure the effects of [society-wide] discrimination, such a showing of the burden by innocent parties is not impermissible."[49]

Similarly, in *Metro Broadcasting* the plaintiff complained that the Federal Communications Commission's policy awarding preferences to minority firms in comparative licensing proceedings handicapped its ability to obtain a license. The Court responded that, "just as we have determined that as part of this Nation's dedication to eradicating racial discrimination, innocent persons may be called upon to bear some of the burdens of the remedy, we similarly find that a congressionally mandated benign race-conscious program that is substantially related to the achievement of an important governmental interest is consistent with equal protection principles so long as it does not impose undue burden on nonminorities."[50]

Were these cases upheld because both were federal programs? While *Fullilove* was decided five to three in favor of the congressionally mandated MBE program, *Metro Broadcasting* was a narrowly split decision. As discussed, a close look at Justice O'Connor's lengthy dissenting view in *Metro Broadcasting*, which was joined by Chief Justice Rehnquist and Justices Scalia and Kennedy makes it clear that the justices in dissent would apply the same strict scrutiny to the federal program as applied to the local program.[51] Justice O'Connor in particular emphasized: "Under the appropriate standard, strict scrutiny, only a compelling interest may support the Government's use of racial classification. . . . Modern equal protection doctrine has recognized only one such interest: remedying the effects of [past] racial discrimination."[52] Similarly, according to O'Connor, the FCC failed to pass muster under the narrowly tailored means test.[53] While it may be argued that federalism was a touchstone dividing between *Croson* on the one hand and *Fullilove* and *Metro Broadcasting* on the other, the dissenting views presented in *Metro Broadcasting* make it difficult to conclude that had O'Connor, for instance, written the opinion in *Metro Broadcasting*, she would then have supported the FCC's decision in principle.

More fundamentally, the discrepancy lies in the fact that the Court has not as yet set forth specific standards of review, allowing it thereby to apply the two-tier framework with a wide latitude. The basic question to address, then, is why the Court applies different standards from case to case.

## THE VIEWS OF INDIVIDUAL JUSTICES

The explanation may be found in the varying judicial views that individual Supreme Court justices hold on the Equal Protection Clause vis-à-vis affirmative action.[54] The position that a justice holds on the bench tends to remain consistent during his or her tenure. In this sense, the level of scrutiny applied to each case is a reflection of how the justices vote and who eventually leads the Court in that particular case. An examination of the voting record (see Table 5.2) reveals that a pattern exists along the level of scrutiny continuum, and further that specific justices can be identified quite predictably with particular standards of review.

The columns in Table 5.2 represent various review standards employed by the Court, and they are arranged on a rough continuum from a strict to liberal application of judicial review. For illustrative purposes, a representative case is selected for the review standard used for that particular case.[55] "Yes" indicates an agreement with the Court opinion, and "No" means a disagreement with the Court opinion. In *Wygant*, for example, Justice Brennan cast a dissenting vote ("No"), arguing that the requirement for prior discrimination was too restrictive. Justice O'Connor, on the other hand, concurred with the Court ("Yes") because she was in agreement with Justice Powell's requirements, including prior discrimination.

As is shown in Table 5.2, three justices—Powell, Brennan, and O'Connor—have been most active in forging Court opinions in affirmative action cases during the last decade. Thus, it is useful to compare the points of their difference, and how others have responded or reacted to these views.

### The Powell Position

The review standard Justice Powell preferred was standard II in our formulation—as he articulated it in *Wygant*, the Court must insist upon "some showing of prior discrimination by the governmental unit before allowing limited use of racial classification in order to remedy such dis-

**Table 5.2**
**The Voting Pattern on Key Affirmative Action Decisions**

| | Judicial Standards of Review | | | |
|---|---|---|---|---|
| Justices | PL/PD *(Croson)* | LQ/PD *(Wygant)* | PL/MI *(Johnson)* | BQ/SD *(Metro)* |
| Rehnquist | Yes | Yes | No | No |
| Scalia | Yes | | No | No |
| Kennedy | Yes | | | No |
| White | Yes | Yes | No | Yes |
| O'Connor | **Yes** | Yes | Yes | No |
| Powell | | **Yes** | Yes | |
| Stevens | Yes | No | Yes | Yes |
| Brennan | No | No | **Yes** | **Yes** |
| Blackmun | No | No | Yes | Yes |
| Marshall | No | No | Yes | Yes |

"Yes" means agreement, and "No"means disagreement with the majority of the Court.
Bold "Yes" indicates the author of the Court opinion.
PL/PD is a plus factor under prior discrimination; LQ/PD is a limited quota under prior
discrimination; PL/MI is a plus factor under manifest imbalance; and BQ/SD is a
benign quota even under society-wide discrimination.

crimination."[56] Standard II represents the centrist position in the recent
U.S. Supreme Court. A close look reveals that this was an extension of
Powell's earlier view expressed in *Bakke* and reiterated in *Fullilove*. In
*Bakke*, Powell argued that in order to justify the use of a suspect classification the states must demonstrate "specific instances of racial discrimination."[57] Similarly, in his concurring opinion in *Fullilove*, Powell wrote
that "the governmental body that attempts to impose a race-conscious
remedy must have the authority to act in response to identified discrimination," and the body "must make findings that demonstrate the existence of
illegal discrimination."[58]

The emphasis on prior discrimination has been supported by those wishing to apply the stricter standard of review, including Chief Justice Rehnquist and Justices Scalia, White, O'Connor, and Kennedy. But unlike Powell, who does support the use of a limited classification, these other justices (with the possible exception of White) have continued to insist on the strict scrutiny standard and to reject the use of a limited quota even as a means to redress past wrongs. These justices favored of a more restricted, race-neutral alternative such as the use of race (or gender) as a plus factor at best; no preference at all would be their generally preferred position. In this respect, Justice Kennedy's concurring opinion in *Croson* seems to sum up the position well: "[T]he strict scrutiny standard will operate in a manner generally consistent with the imperative of race neutrality, because it forbids the use of even narrowly drawn racial classifications except as a last resort."[59] Justices Brennan, Blackmun, Marshall, and Stevens—who represent the liberal wing of the Court—have taken the opposite position, arguing that the requirement of prior discrimination is too restrictive to be practical. They have insisted that the Court permit a "remedial use of race, including a benign racial classification . . . if it serves important governmental objectives."[60] Clearly then, Justice Powell's position— standard II—has remained in the center of the affirmative action debate. His voting record (as presented in Table 5.3 below) is consistent with this observation.

As Table 5.3 shows, *Paradise*, *Sheet Metal Workers*, and *Firefighters* all satisfied the criteria Powell laid down in *Wygant*. Justices Rehnquist, White, and O'Connor agreed with Powell in *Wygant* as it required the showing of prior discrimination, but they disagreed with the Court in these other three cases entailing the use of even limited quotas. Although Justice O'Connor concurred with the Court in *Firefighters*, her support was based not so much on standard II grounds but on the application of Title VII Section 706(g), which deals with benefits accruing to nonvictims of the emmployer's discriminatory practice. For Justices Brennan, Marshall, Blackmun, and Stevens, *Paradise*, *Sheet Metal Workers*, and *Firefighters* more than satisfied their preferred standard so they all voted with Justice Powell. This seems to be where the four justices and Justice Powell have shared a common ground.

### The Brennan Position

Past society-wide discrimination is a theory that presumes that everybody is tainted one way or another by the undesirable effects of discrimination.[61] The question is whether this general concept can amount

**Table 5.3**
**Justice Powell and Other Justices on Model III Decisions**

| Justices | Wygant | Paradise | Sheet Metal | Firefighters |
|----------|--------|----------|-------------|--------------|
| | Limited Quota used under Prior Discrimination | | | |
| Burger* | Yes | | No | No |
| Rehnquist | Yes | No | No | No |
| Scalia | No | | | |
| White | Yes | No | No | No |
| O'Connor | Yes | No | No | Yes |
| Powell* | Yes | Yes | Yes | Yes |
| Stevens | No | Yes | Yes | Yes |
| Brennan* | No | **Yes** | **Yes** | **Yes** |
| Blackmun | No | Yes | Yes | Yes |
| Marshall | No | Yes | Yes | Yes |

Justices* now retired.
"Yes" means concurring with the Court; and "No" dissenting.
"Yes" in bold type indicates the opinion was delivered by the justice in the left column.

to a compelling interest. Justice Brennan and his liberal colleagues—Justices Marshall, Blackmun, and Stevens—have taken a view that eradicating past societal discrimination is an "important governmental objective," and that this public policy objective should be sufficient for a compelling state interest. In his dissenting opinion in *Wygant* Justice Marshall insisted that "the remedial use of race is permissible if it serves important govern-mental objectives and is substantially related to achievement of those objectives."[62] Note that five years later in *City of Richmond v. Croson Co.* (1989), Justice O'Connor spoke for the Court majority, declaring that while "Congress may identify and redress the effects of society-wide discrimination . . . the States and their political subdivisions" may not. To this Justice Marshall rebuked the Court: "Nothing whatever in the legis-lative history of either the Fourteenth Amendment or the Civil Rights Acts even remotely suggests that the States are foreclosed from furthering the fundamental purpose of equal opportunity to which the Amendment and those Acts are addressed."[63]

Within this general framework, Justice Brennan and his liberal col-leagues have embraced a liberal position that the requirement of a com-pelling state interest can be met by a showing of society-wide past discrimination.[64] The society-wide past discrimination also is manifested in a racial (or gender) imbalance in traditionally segregated job cate-gories.[65] With respect to the type of remedies, they believed that the Constitution would permit the use of racial classifications not only in a very limited manner but also benignly as an instrument to advance public policy objectives. Clearly then, the upper limit for Justice Brennan was standard IX—a benign quota under the condition of society-wide past discrimination.

The affirmative action decisions that Justice Brennan has delivered during the past decade fit well in the standard IX formula. In *Johnson v. Transportation Agency* (1987), Justice Brennan, speaking for the majority, upheld the Santa Clara County decision because the county more than satisfied the upper limit of standard IX—it had used gender only as a plus factor and sought justification on the basis of a manifest imbalance. In *Firefighters v. City of Cleveland, Sheet Metal Workers v. EEOC,* and *U.S. v. Paradise,* in which Brennan led the Court, he had no apparent need to invoke the manifest imbalance theory. The agencies had already met even a more stringent condition—they had shown prior illegal discrimination. In *Metro Broadcasting Inc. v. Federal Communications Commission,* in which Justice Brennan again led the Court, as his last decision before retirement, Brennan endorsed the FCC's policies awarding preferences to minorities in comparative licensing proceedings on the basis of the society-wide discrimination theory. Brennan wrote: "We hold that benign race-conscious measures mandated by Congress—even if those measures are not 'remedial' in the sense of being designed to compensate victims of past governmental or societal discrimination—are constitutionally per-missible to the extent that they serve important governmental objectives within the powers of Congress and are substantially related to achievement of those objectives."[66]

## The O'Connor Position

Justice O'Connor's position presents a third alternative in affirmative action. O'Connor's position is complicated (and ambivalent at times) as it moves away from Powell's centrist position to a stricter scrutiny standard, possibly standard I in our formulation. O'Connor made her position clear in several dissenting opinions filed in the past and most recently in *Croson*, in which she wrote the Court opinion. O'Connor maintains that a race-conscious remedy can be justified by identifiable past discrimination by the entity involved and that the remedy must be limited to preferential consideration on a case-by-case approach.[67] O'Connor has been adamantly opposed to the use of a fixed number or percentage or any plan that is intended to maintain a racial balance.[68] In *Croson*, O'Connor rejected the city's plan not only because the city failed to prove identifiable past discrimination but also because it used a fixed quota, which in her opinion was an act of "outright balancing."[69]

Justice O'Connor's position does not reject all forms of remedial action. In this regard, O'Connor appears to maintain some distance from Justices Rehnquist, Scalia, and Kennedy. While Kennedy insists on race-neutral measures, Rehnquist and Scalia seem to reject the consideration of race altogether in employment decisions. While concurring with the Court in *Croson*, Justice Scalia still admonished the Court: "I do not agree, however, with the Court's dicta that, despite the 14th Amendment, State and local governments may in some circumstances discriminate on the basis of race in order (in a broad sense) to 'ameliorate' the effects of past discrimination."[70] *Johnson v. Transportation Agency* seems to be a deviation from O'Connor's charted course. Here, O'Connor concurred with the Court, stating that the employer could legitimately "take sex or race into account" in promotion decisions under certain circumstances. This is consistent with her judicial view. What was inconsistent about her position in *Johnson* was that she endorsed the manifest imbalance theory that she adamantly rejected earlier in *Sheet Metal Workers* and later in *Croson* and *Metro Broadcasting*.[71] In *Metro Broadcasting* she protested: "Under the appropriate standard, strict scrutiny, only a compelling interest may support the Government's use of racial classification." O'Connor added: "Modern equal protection doctrine has recognized only one such interest: remedying the effects of [past discrimination]."[72]

**SUMMARY AND CONCLUSION**

In spite of the fact that since *Bakke* the Court has come to a general agreement that affirmative action decisions are to be reviewed by a two-pronged standard—a compelling interest and narrowly-tailored means—in the last decade the Court has neither operationally defined these review standards nor agreed on how strictly and precisely it should apply them. Except for the trammeling effects on innocent third parties that it considers constitutionally impermissible, the Court has been ambivalent toward affirmative action policy. While the Court insists on the application of strict scrutiny, it at times relaxes the strict scrutiny standard in favor of a more liberal application. Accordingly, the Court has been vacillating in its approach to affirmative action. In this chapter we have seen the Court shifting its review standards in at least five different ways:

1.  Race (or gender) may be used legitimately as a plus factor as a means to remedy identifiable prior discrimination (*City of Richmond v. Croson*, 1989);

2.  A limited racial (or gender) classification (quota) may be used as a means to remedy identifiable prior discrimination (*UC Regents v. Bakke*, 1978; *Wygant v. Jackson Bd of Education*, 1985; *U.S. v. Paradise*, 1987);

3.  Race (or gender) may be considered as a plus in an effort to eliminate a manifest imbalance or to remedy prior discrimination (*Johnson v. Transportation Agency*, 1987);

4.  A limited racial (or gender) classification (quota) may be used as a means to eliminate a manifest imbalance or prior discrimination (*Wygant v. Jackson Bd of Education*, 1985; *Johnson v. Transportation Agency*, 1987); and

5.  A benign limited racial (or gender) classification (quota) may be used as a means to accomplish important governmental objectives (i.e., eradicating society-wide past discrimination) (*Fullilove v. Klutznick*, 1980; *Metro Broadcasting v. FCC*, 1990).

The existence of these variable standards underscores the fact that the Court has not as yet formulated a coherent review policy toward affirmative action. Meanwhile, the Court has been issuing conflicting standards, seriously complicating the job of public administration. Why has the Court been so ambivalent? The argument presented in this chapter is that the two-tier analytic framework used by the Court to review affirmative action is not a systematic test but largely a statement of values open to interpretation. As a result, the framework has been unequally applied from case to case, depending on which justice is able to forge the Court opinion at a particular time.

On closer view, three justices—Powell, Brennan, and O'Connor—have been most active in shaping the Court opinions during the past decade, in particular with respect to the application of the two-tier analytic framework. With respect to the compelling interest requirement, Justice Powell insisted—and Justices Burger, Rehnquist, White, and O'Connor, agreed—that affirmative action programs must be designed only to correct prior discrimination by the entity itself. Thus, when Powell led the Court in *Wygant* and O'Connor in *Croson*, the Court adhered to this requirement. On the liberal side, Justice Brennan broadened the scope of justification—and Justices Marshall, Blackmun, and Stevens endorsed—to include not only manifest imbalance in traditionally segregated job categories but also society-wide discrimination demonstrated in the past. The Brennan position has been that affirmative action programs may be properly implemented to eliminate a manifest imbalance or in pursuit of important governmental objectives designed to eradicate society-wide discrimination. This framework has been the basis for endorsing *United Steelworkers*, *Johnson*, and *Metro Broadcasting*—in all of which Brennan led the Court.

The choice of means has been divided in three ways, primarily among Justices Powell, Brennan, and O'Connor. O'Connor's position has been that affirmative action plans must be limited to preferential consideration (race and gender as plus factors) on a case-by-case approach; she has been vigorously opposed to the idea of even a limited quota system. While Powell has been open to the idea of a narrowly drawn quota system with built-in safeguards, Brennan went further to embrace the idea of benign classification—a broad (as opposed to narrowly tailored) classification intended to accomplish important governmental objectives. *Metro Broadcasting* represents this position.

Justices Powell and Brennan—the architects of the constitutional theory of affirmative action—have retired from the bench. Inasmuch as a Court opinion is shaped by a coalition of ideas and judicial philosophies on the bench, and inasmuch as the judicial standards of review contain the elements of ambiguity, the future of affirmative action will be fashioned principally by the value preferences of those on the bench and not by a particular principle. In this connection, what remains constant in the equation is Justice O'Connor's position—that affirmative action programs must be narrowly tailored or restricted to only a plus consideration on a case-by-case approach and that such programs must be justified by identifiable past discrimination. Thus, the future Court under Chief Justice Rehnquist is mostly likely to embark upon a strict scrutiny path.

From the viewpoint of public policy, the affirmative action debate will inevitably change in focus, gradually moving away from the idea of quotas to a case-by-case approach. The challenge here will be to structure affirmative action policy in a way that is consistent with the requirement of equal protection. While this may present a formidable challenge to public administrators, the undertaking should be more palatable intellectually than the previous approach. If strict scrutiny holds that merit is the only constitutionally acceptable employment criterion, affirmative action debate may have to be focused on the concept of merit, attempting to redefine it in a way that is not going to be disadvantageous to a particular class. That may well require reconceptualizing the word "merit" broadly in terms of what a person is capable of contributing to his or her employer and the larger community in which he or she is a part.

## NOTES

1. 438 U.S. 265 (1978).
2. 100 S. Ct. 2785 (1980).
3. 476 U.S. 267 (1985).
4. John Nalbandian, "The U.S. Supreme Court's 'Consensus' on Affirmative Action," *Public Administration Review* 49 (January/February 1989), 38–45.
5. Mitchell F. Rice, "Government Set-Asides, Minority Business Enterprises, and the Supreme Court," *Public Administration Review* 51 (March/April 1991), 114–122.
6. 109 S. Ct. 706 (1989).
7. 58 LW 5053 (1990).
8. David H. Rosenbloom, "The Declining Salience of Affirmative Action in Federal Management," *Review of Public Personnel Administration* 4 (Summer 1984), 31–40.
9. *Metro Broadcasting*, 5070.
10. 106 S. Ct. 3019, 3052 (1986).
11. 107 S. Ct. 1053 (1987).
12. Ibid., 1080.
13. 99 S. Ct. 2721 (1979).
14. *Johnson*, 1471.
15. *Croson*, 735.
16. Ibid., 752.
17. Ibid., 752.
18. Alan H. Goldman, *Justice and Reverse Discrimination* (Princeton: Princeton University Press, 1979). See also William Kelso, "From Bakke to Fullilove: Has the Supreme Court Finally Settled the Affirmative Action Controversy?" *Review of Public Personnel Administration* 1 (1980), 57–74, and Rosenbloom.

19. With the retirement of Justices Brennan and Marshall, who have been the most outspoken advocates for a wide range of race-conscious remedies, the Court in the future is likely to move toward stricter scrutiny in affirmative action reviews. Meanwhile, public administrators may have to make affirmative action decisions without clear direction from the Court.

20. After two full years of wrangling with the Bush administration, on October 30, 1991, Congress passed a new civil rights law called the Civil Rights Act of 1991. A cursory review suggests that the 1991 law is a heavily compromised piece of legislation and that the legislative record is filled with conflicting expectations. It is unlikely that the new law will alter in any significant way the views of the justices in the present Court. Nor will it help to clarify the present state of the law for public administrators. See *Congressional Record*, Senate Hearings, October 25, 30, 1991, pp. S15445–S15512.

21. *New York Times*, "Cavazos Quits as Education Chief Amid Pressure From White House," December 13, 1990, A1.

22. Jill Zuchman, "Minority Scholarship Fracas Raises a Sensitive Issue," *Congressional Quarterly*, 48, 50 (December 15, 1990), 41–43.

23. In this connection, on December 13, 1990, the White House asked Education Secretary Lauro F. Cavazos to step down.

24. *New York Times*, "Under the Rug: Minority Scholarships," February 6, 1991, A20.

25. See Justice Stevens' concurring opinion in *Johnson v. Transportation Agency*, 1459. "Prior to 1978," Stevens pointed out, "the Court construed Title VII as an absolute blanket prohibition against discrimination which neither required nor permitted discriminatory preference for any group, minority or majority." "The Court endorsed the neutral approach," he added, as laid down by *Griggs v. Duke Power* in 1971. "In *Bakke* in 1978 and again in *Steelworkers v. Weber* in 1979," admitted Stevens, "a majority of the Court interpreted the antidiscriminatory strategy of the statute in a fundamentally different way."

26. *Bakke*, 291.

27. Ibid., 299.

28. Ibid., 305–315.

29. See Justice Marshall's dissenting opinion in *Wygant v. Jackson Board of Education*, 302. Marshall argued that "remedial use of race is permissible if it serves important governmental objectives and is substantially related to achievement of those objectives." Justices Brennan and Blackmun joined Justice Marshall's view. In a separate dissenting opinion, Justice Stevens also maintained that "public purpose transcends the harm to innocent third parties." See also Ralph A. Rossum, *American Behavioral Scientist*, 28 (July/August 1985) 785–806; "*Plessy, Brown*, and the Reverse Discrimination Cases," (1980: 23–55).

30. See Brennan's separate opinion in *University of California Regents v. Bakke*, 359; and *United Steelworkers v. Weber*, and Justice Marshall's dissenting opinion in *City of Richmond v. Croson Co.*

31. See Justice Rehnquist's dissenting view in *United Steelworkers v. Weber*, 2737; Justice Stewart's dissenting view in *Fullilove v. Klutznick*, 2798; and Justice Scalia's concurring opinion in *City of Richmond v. Croson Co.*, 735.

32. See Justice Powell's opinion in *University of California Regents v. Bakke*, 307; his concurring opinion in *Fullilove v. Klutznick*, 2875; and his opinion for the Court in *Wygant v. Jackson Board of Education*, 274. See also Justice O'Connor's opinion for the Court in *City of Richmond v. Croson Co.*, 724.

33. See Justice O'Connor's dissenting view in *U.S. v. Paradise*, 1080. She wrote: "Because the Court adopts a standardless view of 'narrowly tailored' far less stringent than that required by strict scrutiny, I dissent."

34. *Johnson*, 1464.

35. *Wygant*, 275.

36. *Croson*, 729.

37. *Wygant*, 282.

38. Ibid., 283.

39. 416 U.S. 313 (1974).

40. *Wygant*, 283.

41. Ibid., 283.

42. See *Sheet Metal Workers v. EEOC*, 3052. Local 28 of the sheet metal workers' union showed the evidence of "persistent or egregious discrimination" against blacks and Hispanic individuals in violation of Title VII, thereby satisfying the prior discrimination requirement. The consent decree also was believed to be a temporary measure and an efficacious choice. The remaining issue then was the plan's impact on innocent third parties.

43. *Firefighters v. City of Cleveland*, 478 U.S. 501 (1986).

44. *Firefighters v. Stotts*.

45. *Fullilove*, 2278.

46. *Croson*, 729.

47. *Johnson*, 1465.

48. Ibid., 1456.

49. *Fullilove*, 2278.

50. *Metro Broadcasting*, 5066.

51. Ibid., 5069.

52. Ibid., 5070.

53. Ibid., 5073.

54. See Nalbandian, "Supreme Court's Consensus"; Rice, "Government Set-Asides."

55. While standards I, IV, and VII are represented by the same cases depicted in Figure 5.3, standard II is represented by *Wygant* and standard XII by *Metro Broadcasting*. *Wygant* is considered representative of standard II in that the Court insisted on the showing of prior discrimination, which the Jackson School Board could not provide. In *Paradise*, *Firefighters v. Cleveland*, and *Sheet Metal Workers*, however, the employers had met the requirement of showing prior discrimination, and the Court believed that the evidence was more than sufficient to meet the strict scrutiny test. Standard IX is represented by *Metro Broadcasting* because the case is recent and shows the fuller dimensions of the controversy.

56. *Wygant*, 274.

57. *Bakke*, 307.

58. *Fullilove*, 2784.

59. *Croson*, 734.

60. *Wygant*, 302.

61. *Bakke*, 365.

62. *Wygant*, 302.

63. *Croson*, 754.

64. *Bakke*, 328.

65. *United Steelworkers*, 2728.

66. *Metro Broadcasting*, 5057.
67. *Paradise*, 1080–1082.
68. *Johnson*, 1462.
69. *Croson*, 729.
70. Ibid., 734.
71. Some argue that the standard of review for sex discrimination is subject to less strict scrutiny than racial classifications. See Norman Vieira (1990): 110–127.
72. See Justice O'Connor's dissenting view in *Metro Broadcasting*, 5070. In the passage cited, O'Connor used the term "racial discrimination" rather than "past discrimination." But in the context of the entire paragraph it is clear that she meant past discrimination. To quote the relevant part of the paragraph: "First, it too casually extends the justifications that might support racial classifications, beyond that of remedying past discrimination."

# 6

# *Pay Equity and a Battle of the Sexes*

The present controversy over pay inequity between men and women in employment has been unnecessarily limited to a debate on comparable worth. This obfuscates a more general Title VII approach[1] to pay disparities because comparable worth, despite its popularity in the literature, represents only a small part of many complex legal avenues by which discrimination is challenged in practice. Indeed, most recent gender discrimination lawsuits do not neatly fit in the comparable worth framework. It would make more sense if attention were focused instead on what kinds of policies, practices, or nonaction are likely to be in violation of Title VII. Whether comparable worth per se creates a cause of action under Title VII is an inquiry without much practical significance because most recently the U.S. Court of Appeals for the Ninth Circuit once again refused to recognize comparable worth as a viable legal theory in *Spaulding v. University of Washington* (1984)[2] and *AFSCME v. State of Washington* (1985).[3]

This chapter identifies three Title VII grounds on which gender-based wage discrimination claims are litigated in lower federal courts: (1) unequal pay for equal work, (2) unequal pay for work of comparable worth, and (3) unjustified pay disparity for comparable work. Equal work means jobs, performance of which require equal or substantially equal skills, effort, responsibility and working conditions. Comparable worth measures the worth of jobs to the employer, regardless of the differences in their qualifications. Comparable or similar work refers to a classification of positions or individuals who are similarly situated for purposes of compensation, such as college professors of different disciplines. We begin with the two contrasting views articulated by U.S. Supreme Court Justices Brennan and Rehnquist in *County of Washington v. Gunther* (1981).[4] In the Court's majority opinion, Justice Brennan wrote that gender-based wage discrimination claims are actionable under Title VII—without having to meet the equal work standard required by the Equal Pay Act of 1963. Justice Rehnquist, however, insisted in his dissenting view that Title VII claimants must first meet the equal work standard. Rehnquist also rejected comparable worth as a legal theory. This chapter examines how these two contrasting views contributed to shaping lower federal court responses in gender-based wage discrimination claims. While in respect to comparable worth lower courts have been overwhelmingly on the side of Rehnquist's dissenting view,[5] Brennan's view is gaining new life thanks to *Bazemore v. Friday* (1986)[6]—another landmark decision on the subject of discrimination. In *Bazemore*, the Supreme Court recognized that multiple regression statistical data can be acceptable circumstantial evidence of discrimination, thereby making it possible that a Title VII claimant might use the statistical technique to raise the presumption of gender discrimination on the basis of data as to similarly situated employees or comparable work.

## LEGAL THEORY OF GENDER DISCRIMINATION

Relevant to the problem of pay inequity in employment are two statutes: the Equal Pay Act of 1963, which was an amendment to the Fair Labor Standard Act of 1938,[7] and Title VII of the Civil Rights Act of 1964, as amended in 1972, the relevant parts of which are contained in two subsections—703(a) and 703(h).[8] The legal theory of gender discrimination in employment compensation cases centers on the relationship between these two pieces of legislation, as the U.S. Supreme Court articulated in the *Gunther* case; lower courts continue to interpret this ruling on a case-by-case basis.

The Equal Pay Act, which focuses exclusively on gender, makes it unlawful for an employer to pay unequal wages for equal work as defined in terms of equal skill, effort, responsibility, and working conditions. However, the law provides four exceptions to this rule in which unequal payments can be made to accommodate: (1) a seniority system, (2) a merit system, (3) a system that measures earnings by quantity or quality of production, or (4) any factor other than gender. Section 703(a) of Title VII, on the other hand, makes no specific reference to the equal work requirements; it simply prohibits discrimination in compensation on the basis of

race, religion, sex, or national origin. Reading these two pieces of legislation alone, therefore, it appears that the two laws are in conflict, because
an employer who may be found liable for wage discrimination under Title
VII may be excused under the Equal Pay Act for the reason of the equal
work principle. *Gunther* exemplified this conflict. Presumably in anticipa-
tion of such conflict, the Eighty-Eighth Congress adopted 703(h), known
as the Bennett Amendment, to acknowledge that employers would be
exempted from Title VII liability if their wage disparities were authorized
by the Equal Pay Act.[9]

As it turned out, the Bennett Amendment was disappointingly unclear,
and the U.S. Supreme Court in *Gunther* took pains to try to determine
which part of the Equal Pay Act the Bennett Amendment intended to
incorporate as part of Title VII—the equal work principle, or only the
four enumerated exceptions to that principle. This is a centrally important question in the legal theory of gender discrimination in employment
compensation, because if the amendment had incorporated only the four
exceptions, Title VII claimants would have no need to prove the equality
of work, thereby effectively circumventing the Equal Pay Act's equal
work requirement. If, on the other hand, the amendment were to have
incorporated the equal work principle, all sex-based wage discrimination
claims under Title VII would first have to meet the equal work requirement. This obviously would make Title VII virtually powerless in
gender-based wage discrimination claims. A more substantive review of
the debate is in order.

In *Gunther*, four discharged female jail matrons sued Washington
County, Oregon under Title VII, complaining that during their tenure as
matrons, the county had paid them lower wages than their male counterparts even though their work was substantially equal to their male
counterparts and that the wage disparity was a consequence of "intentional sex discrimination" that violated Title VII. The U.S. District Court
for the Western District of Washington dismissed the charge on the
ground that the matrons did not perform equal work within the meaning
of the Equal Pay Act. For the claim of intentional sex discrimination, the
district court determined that Title VII was inapplicable because the
plaintiffs had failed to meet the equal work standard set forth by the
Equal Pay Act.

The Ninth Circuit Court of Appeals disagreed with the lower court
ruling, and on certiorari the U.S. Supreme Court held by a narrow
majority—five to four—that the Bennett Amendment did not require that
Title VII claimants meet the Equal Pay Act's equal work standard.[10]
Speaking for the majority, Justice Brennan announced that the Bennett

Amendment merely incorporated the Equal Pay Act's four affirmative defenses into Title VII.[11] Justice Rehnquist, joined by Justices Burger, Stewart, and Powell, on the other hand, argued strenuously against the majority position, insisting that the Bennett Amendment incorporated the equal work standard.[12]

Rehnquist obviously feared that Brennan's view might be taken as an open invitation to comparable worth claims. Thus he explicitly rejected comparable worth as a legal theory, arguing not only that Congress had specifically rejected comparable worth when considering the Equal Pay Act, but also that the same Congress had not changed its mind a year later when considering Title VII.[13] Brennan countered the dissent by stating that the *Gunther* Court was not dealing with the comparable worth doctrine[14] and that the Court was neither endorsing the doctrine nor rejecting it implicitly or explicitly. He merely articulated the Court's position that gender-based wage discrimination claims are actionable under Title VII even if they do not meet the equal work standard. But on what legal basis may a Title VII claimant allege discrimination? Justice Brennan declined to outline "the precise contours" of such lawsuits.[15]

The text is clear that both Justices Brennan and Rehnquist had no disagreement over the meaning and intent of the Equal Pay Act: both concurred that it makes it unlawful for an employer to pay unequal wages for equal work on the basis of gender; that it provides for four affirmative defenses; that it is strictly concerned with the situation of "equal or substantially equal work," not of "comparable worth"; and that the Equal Pay Act focuses specifically on gender-based wage discrimination complaints. The disagreement was simply which of the two statutes should control when the two are found in conflict. If the Equal Pay Act were to supersede Title VII, this unfortunately would mean that the four female guards in *Gunther* and all others similarly situated would have to meet the test of equal work.

For their part, Brennan relied on the language of the Bennett Amendment itself, and Rehnquist relied on the legislative history. Note that Section 703(a) of Title VII makes it unlawful to discriminate on the basis of sex in compensation, but Section 703(h)—the Bennett Amendment—makes it legal to do so if such discrimination is authorized by the provisions of the Equal Pay Act. The puzzle, then, is what the Equal Pay Act had in fact authorized—the equal work standard or the four affirmative defenses. To Brennan it absolutely made no sense to read that the act had authorized the "unequal pay for equal work." The authorization, in his view, had to do with the four exceptions.[16] If the Bennett Amendment had intended to acknowledge the four exceptions only, plaintiffs seeking a remedy under Title VII should be able to do so without worrying about the equal work standard. In this case, the defendant employer must explain that the observed wage disparities were due to the exceptional circumstances authorized by the Equal Pay Act.

Rehnquist's argument was more complex and perhaps may best be read between the lines. He probably would have surmised that the language of the Bennett Amendment is vague and unqualified, making it best not to pursue its literal interpretation. Instead, the amendment was better looked at in the context of the legislative history of the Equal Pay Act.[17] When that act was adopted in 1963, Rehnquist argued, Congress specifically rejected comparable worth in favor of equal work. The same Congress in 1964 could not have changed its mind without even having a debate.[18] The Bennett Amendment, therefore, could not be interpreted as an amendment intended to repeal the equal pay for equal work principle, but one that incorporates the equal work principle into Title VII.[19] Thus, if sex discrimination claims are to be filed under Title VII, Rehnquist insisted, the claimants must show the proof of equal work, not comparable worth.

Two points are central to the purpose here. First, with respect to comparable worth, the Court maintained an ambivalent position by neither endorsing it nor rejecting it as a legal theory. The dissenting justices, however, strenuously opposed the concept. When the two positions are juxtaposed, therefore, it is not likely that the concept will survive in lower courts. Second, the Court did not restrict Title VII claims to the Equal Pay Act, yet it refused to outline the legal basis on which discrimination may be alleged. If the disparate treatment and disparate impact approaches—the main vehicles of Title VII litigation—were applied to gender discrimination, how might the plaintiff raise the presumption of discrimination, as required to establish a prima facie case? The Court left the task to lower courts, at least for the time being.

## PATHS TO SEX DISCRIMINATION CLAIMS

While the *Gunther* Court refused to outline the precise contours of Title VII lawsuits, an examination of lower court cases reveals that Title VII claims with respect to gender-based wage discrimination have proceeded on the basis of three principal grounds: equal work, comparable worth, and comparable work, all of which are premised on the theory of intentional discrimination. On a closer look, this development—and also attendant lower court responses—has been predicated on the Brennan-Rehnquist debate. The reasons for this postulate are further discussed below. Figure 6.1 sketches the paths to Title VII claims based on the theory of intentional discrimination. The paths are constructed to show that all Title VII claims of gender discrimination in pay are required to raise the presumption of intentional discrimination.

**Figure 6.1**
**Critical Paths to Gender Discrimination in Pay**

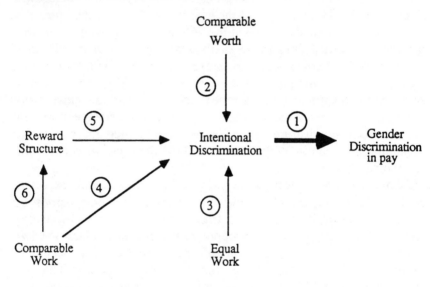

" ———▶ " creates an inference of discrimination

" ━━▶ " means an unlawful behavior.

### Intentional Discrimination

The central thesis of Brennan's view in *Gunther* is that intentional gender discrimination in employment compensation is actionable under Title VII—regardless of the Equal Pay Act. Two types of discrimination traditionally have been recognized under Title VII: disparate treatment and disparate impact. Disparate treatment is overt discrimination in employment, and it involves a discriminatory motive. Disparate impact, on the other hand, occurs from an employer's facially neutral actions that have a discriminatory effect.

The burden of proof is somewhat different under these two approaches. Under the disparate treatment theory established in *McDonnell-Douglas Corp. v. Green* (1973)[20] and later applied in *Texas Dept. of Community Affairs v. Burdine* (1981),[21] the plaintiff has the burden of proving a prima facie case of discrimination by a preponderance of the evidence, for which the plaintiff must show the employer's discriminatory motive.[22] If the plaintiff succeeds in this, the burden shifts to the employer who then must articulate some legitimate, nondiscriminatory reason for the disparate treatment. Business necessity, bona fide occupational qualifications, and the four affirmative defenses set forth by the Equal Pay Act may exemplify legitimate reasons. Assuming that the employer has successfully articulated nondiscriminatory reasons for the disparate treatment, the plaintiff again must show by a preponderance of the evidence that the reasons offered by the employer were not the true reasons but a mere pretext to justify the discrimination.[23]

Under the disparate impact theory the plaintiff need not show the employer's discriminatory motive, but simply challenge that the employer's facially neutral practice—a specific policy or practice—has a disproportionate impact on women or racial minorities.[24] Meeting the 80 percent rule[25] or showing a strong multiple regression effect (e.g., $R^2$ = .80)[26] may be sufficient to meet the preponderance of the evidence requirement. The employer then must articulate a nondiscriminatory reason for the disparate impact, such as legitimate business necessity. As in the disparate treatment theory, the final burden of production falls on the plaintiff, who then must show that the employer's explanation is not bona fide in order to prevail. *Gunther* only dealt with intentional discrimination (path 1), but several lower federal courts in recent years have applied the disparate impact theory to sex discrimination claims.[27]

## Comparable Worth

A comparison of jobs between men and women within a firm or an agency is expressed in numerical terms based on the intrinsic worth of the jobs to the employer. The worth is determined by several abstract qualities or factors such as responsibility, knowledge and skills required, personal contacts, and environmental hazard.[28] The number and types of factors chosen for comparison vary from one employer to another. Justice Rehnquist argued that comparable worth per se provides no legal basis for seeking a remedy, but Justice Brennan's view opened a door to comparable worth via intentional discrimination (path 2).[29]

### Equal Work

Equal work does not necessarily mean identical work; it may be substantially similar work on jobs "the performance of which requires equal skill, effort, and responsibility, and which are performed under similar working conditions."[30] The Equal Pay Act prohibits unequal pay for equal work, excepting the four affirmative defenses. Thanks to the Bennett Amendment, the violation of equal pay for equal work may constitute intentional discrimination under Title VII (path 3).[31] No differences exist between Brennan and Rehnquist on this view.

### Reward Structure

Wage discrimination, intentional or otherwise, may be inferred from the employer's compensation policy itself—its reward system. It is assumed that the employer distributes rewards (e.g., pay increase and promotion) based on certain criteria such as productivity, experience, and the market. In practice, an employer might not have a specific formula.[32] Discrimination may be inferred (path 5) if the reward system is unfairly and discriminatorily applied on the basis of gender, provided that the jobs are essentially similar or comparable, as with college professors in different departments.[33]

### Comparable Work

Whereas equal work means substantial equality in skills, effort, responsibility, and working conditions, the term comparable work is used by courts to refer to similar work or those who are similarly situated.[34] College professors of different disciplines may not be considered as performing equal work,[35] but they may be considered as engaged in similar and comparable work.[36] Since the term comparable is not the same as equal, the plaintiff may statistically demonstrate the pure effect of discrimination by systematically accounting for the relevant differences.[37] While Rehnquist would not extend the scope of Title VII liability to comparable work as he insisted on limiting it to the equal work standard (path 4), Brennan's view is broad enough to permit construction of a prima facie case on the basis of comparable work (path 6).

## LITIGATED LAWSUITS IN FEDERAL COURTS

Title VII claims litigated from 1982 to early 1988 both in federal district and appeals courts were reviewed for this study. This research identified a total of sixty-four lawsuits of gender discrimination in employment compensation—thirty-nine district court cases and twenty-five appellate court cases. The review covered the *Federal Supplement*, volumes 519 to 685, and the *Federal Reporter, Second Series*, volumes 669 to 850. The cases are listed in Appendixes 6-A and 6-B. Tables 6.1 and 6.2 show an overall pattern of distribution by the years under observation.[38]

**Table 6.1**
**Title VII Claims of Gender Discrimination in Pay Litigated in Federal District Courts from 1982 to 1988***

| Basis of Claims | 1982-1983 | 1984-1985 | 1986-1988 | Total | Percent |
|---|---|---|---|---|---|
| Equal Work | 4 | 9 | 6 | 19 | 51.4 |
| Comparable Worth | 3 | 1 | 1 | 5 | 12.8 |
| Comparable Work | 5 | 5 | 3 | 13 | 35.1 |
| Total | 12 | 15 | 10 | 37 | 100.0 |

**Federal Supplement*, Volume 685 (August 1988) is the last volume included here.

**Table 6.2**
**Title VII Claims of Gender Discrimination in Pay Litigated in Circuit Courts from 1982 to 1988***

| Basis of Claims | 1982-1983 | 1984-1985 | 1986-1988 | Total | Percent |
|---|---|---|---|---|---|
| Equal Work | 4 | 2 | 10 | 16 | 64.0 |
| Comparable Worth | 0 | 1 | 1 | 2 | 8.0 |
| Comparable Work | 1 | 1 | 5 | 7 | 28.0 |
| Total | 6 | 4 | 15 | 25 | 100.0 |

**Federal Reporter, 2nd Series*, Volume 850 (August 1988) is the last volume examined here.

The data show that the distribution of Title VII claims is similar between district courts and appeals courts, with equal work claims representing a majority of gender discrimination claims (51.4 percent at the district court level and 64 percent at the appellate court level). Comparable worth claims represented only a minor part, 13.5 percent at the district court level and 8 percent at the appellate level, respectively, which were then followed by a near complete eclipse in the aftermath of *AFSCME* in 1985. Equal work claims and claims based on comparable work, on the other hand, have been relatively on the increase. Explanations for this trend are noted in the following discussion of the development of case law.

## Equal Work Claims

The central task in equal work claims is to prove that the female plaintiff has performed equal or substantially equal work to that of males, as defined in the Equal Pay Act. What precisely constitutes substantially equal work is subject to much legal wrangling. Even though the complaint involves one employment position, the work may not be considered equal or substantially equal to an earlier position if the employer modified the new position by adding or subtracting duties and responsibilities.[39]

The concept of comparable work also cannot be substituted for the term substantially equal work. In *Spaulding v. University of Washington,* (1984)[40] the nursing faculty appealed to the U.S. Court of Appeals for the Ninth Circuit, arguing that the University of Washington violated the Equal Pay Act by paying them unequal wages for work substantially equal to that performed by male faculty members in other parts of the university. Circuit Judge Wallace upheld the lower court decision by observing that "because a comparable work standard cannot be substituted for an equal work standard, evidence of comparable work, although not necessarily irrelevant in proving discrimination under some alternative theory, will not alone be sufficient to establish a prima facie case."[41] In *Horner v. Mary Institute* (1981)[42] jobs of two physical education teachers were determined to be superficially identical but not substantially equal.[43] In order to meet the equal work standard, Judge Wallace in *Spaulding* emphasized that "[a]ctual job performance and content, rather than job descriptions, titles or classifications, is determinative." For each claim that jobs are substantially equal, he noted, the equality "necessarily must be determined on a case-by-case basis."[44]

Once the presumption of discrimination has been established, the burden shifts to the employer who then must articulate (not persuade) legitimate, nondiscriminatory reasons for the pay disparity. The Equal Pay

Act and the Bennett Amendment provide that wage differentials may be maintained without violating law if they were a result of the application of a seniority system, a merit system, a system that measures earnings by quantity or quality of production, or any other factor other than sex. The fourth factor—"any other factor other than sex"—is generally referred to as a market system. Federal courts all maintain that Title VII does not fault the free market system as "a suspect enterprise."[45] Even though initially successful in establishing a prima facie case, therefore, most equal work claims in the past have been lost on grounds of the market factor.[46]

## Comparable Worth Claims

Before *Gunther*, federal courts that considered comparable worth claims insisted that gender-based wage discrimination claims be judged exclusively under the Equal Pay Act standard, thereby refusing to grant a cause of action under Title VII.[47] After *Gunther*, however, some district courts attempted to recognize comparable worth claims under Title VII, but no opinion became persuasively authoritative.[48] In 1983 a major controversy developed when District Judge Tanner for the Western District of Washington at Tacoma ruled that the state of Washington violated Title VII when it failed to implement the comparable worth schedule recommended by the state legislature. In this historic lawsuit, two unions—the American Federation of State, County, and Municipal Employees (AFSCME) and the Washington Federation of State Employees—filed a gender-based wage discrimination claim on behalf of approximately fifteen thousand state employees in job categories predominantly held by women. The AFSCME alleged that the state legislature had earlier adopted a comparable worth policy with two bills, but the governor failed to implement the new compensation policy without legitimate and overriding business reasons. While the ruling was about to cost the state more than $700 million in back pay and salary adjustments, the state appealed, and the Ninth Circuit reversed the lower court ruling.

Circuit Judge Kennedy did not think that the plaintiffs could establish a prima facie case of intentional discrimination because the state failed to implement a comparable worth program, which Title VII does not even recognize.[49] In his view, the legislative history of the Bennett Amendment was not sufficient to draw any conclusion about the scope of Title VII liability in gender discrimination. Nor did the U.S. Supreme Court in *Gunther*, he noted, determine how such lawsuits might proceed. Kennedy went further to reject the disparate impact argument—AFSCME's second claim—by stating that the argument should be applied to cases that challenge "a specific, clearly delineated employment practice applied at a single point in the job selection process," such as height, high school diploma, or arrest record.[50] The disparate impact theory should not be applied to cases challenging wide-ranging employment discrimination.

Similarly, in *International Union, U.A.W. v. State of Michigan* (1987)[51] the union attempted to construct a prima facie case of intentional discrimination based on the fact that the state had not consistently paid the female positions the same as the male positions that are evaluated to have the same factor scores or the same value to the employer.[52] The court gently reminded that although the plaintiffs "carefully avoided the term at the trial, what [they] have presented is a comparable worth case." Citing *AFSCME*, the court simply refused to consider the complaint.

Even though *Gunther* did not recognize comparable worth per se, *Gunther* did not reject the possibility that Title VII claimants could somehow show an inference of intentional discrimination based on comparable worth. In *American Nurses' Association v. State of Illinois* (1986),[53] where the state prevailed, Circuit Judge Posner surmised that intentional discrimination may be inferred from comparable worth if the employer had "knowingly" and "willfully" failed to take a needed action.[54] This would mean that the employer "has declined to act on the result of the comparable worth study not because it prefers to pay . . . market wages but because it thinks men deserve to be paid more than women."[55] The speculation remains to be tested.

## COMPARABLE WORK AND MULTIPLE REGRESSION

All gender discrimination claimants under Title VII have a monumental task of proving discrimination—monumental in that the burden of proof falls on the plaintiff at all times. For this reason, when comparable worth was determined not to provide a legal basis under Title VII, the outlook for gender-based wage discrimination claims under Title VII did indeed look hopeless.[56]

A dramatic shift in Title VII law occurred in 1986, when the U.S. Supreme Court, in *Bazemore v. Friday*—a case involving racial discrimination in employment—formally recognized the viability of the multiple regression analysis in establishing a prima facie case of discrimination. Under *Bazemore*, with statistical evidence, plaintiffs can make their prima facie case, raising a presumption of discrimination by a preponderance of the evidence or, better yet, showing that "racial discrimination [is] the [employer's] standard operating procedure—the regular rather than the unusual practice."[57]

Bazemore and other black employees at North Carolina State University alleged that although the university's Agricultural Extension Service had ended discriminatory treatment of blacks since 1972,[58] it failed to make a necessary salary adjustment for them and, as a result, their salaries continued to reflect the pre-Title ("pre-act") discrimination. The plaintiffs used a multiple regression analysis to explain that a portion of the wage disparity between black and other employees was due to the pre-act discrimination. Ruling in favor of the plaintiffs, Justice Brennan, speaking for a unanimous Court, admonished the court of appeals:

> The Court of Appeals erred in stating that petitioners' regression analyses were "unacceptable as evidence of discrimination," because they did not include "all measurable variables thought to have an effect on salary level." The court's view of the evidentiary value of the regression analyses was plainly incorrect. While the omission of variables from a regression analysis may render the analysis less probative than it otherwise might be, it can hardly be said, absent some other infirmity, that an analysis which accounts for the major factors "must be considered unacceptable as evidence of discrimination." Normally, failure to include variables will affect the analysis' probativeness, not its admissibility.[59]

Until 1975 no Title VII cases had used a regression analysis.[60] Since then, multiple regression has gradually entered the courtroom. In *Vuyanich v. Republic National Bank of Dallas* (1980)[61] the district court accepted multiple regression as circumstantial evidence to establish a prima facie case even though the model, in the trial judge's view, was not "perfectly designed." Similarly, in *EEOC v. Federal Reserve Bank of Richmond* (1983)[62] the Court of Appeals for the Fourth Circuit held that "[s]tatistics, when properly authenticated, constitute an accepted form of circumstantial evidence of employment discrimination and may sometimes be sufficient to establish . . . prima facie proof of discrimination."[63]

The advantage of using a regression analysis in disparate impact cases is its ability to systematically factor out the effect of several variables simultaneously and to isolate the effect of the gender variable. Typically, the plaintiff constructs what some writers call the "human capital equation," in which all variables potentially affecting wage determination are "regressed" on the observed wage disparity.[64] Education ($X_1$), experience ($X_2$), merit ($X_3$), market factor ($X_4$), and gender ($X_5$), for example, may enter the equation as they are assumed to have an influence on the wage level (Y). Thus, $Y = a + b_1X_1 \ b_2X_2 + b_3X_3 + b_4X_4 + b_5X_5$, where "a" is the constant dollars and the "b's" are the coefficients for the explanatory variables, respectively. Assuming that the model fits well with the data, that is, that there is "goodness of fit," the plaintiff might wish to show that even where the effects of all other variables have been controlled for, the gender variable ($X_5$) still contributes significantly to the admitted wage disparity, both substantively and statistically.

In *AFSCME* the Ninth Circuit reaffirmed the earlier case law that the employer could not be held responsible for discriminatory effects of the free market.[65] In *Denny v. Westfield State College* (1987),[66] where the female faculty alleged on the basis of a multiple regression analysis that because of gender, they were paid less than the similarly situated male faculty at Westfield, the college attempted to dismiss the charge based on yet another regression analysis, suggesting that the disparities had to do with departmental affiliation—a type of market force. The court refused to accept the college's argument, pointing out that the Westfield regression model, which included the departmental variable, still did not fully account for the wage disparities in all years studied. The moral of *Denny* is that while market-based discrimination was found acceptable in *AFSCME*, the multiple regression analysis in *Denny* demonstrated that the market factor is not necessarily an air-tight defense for discrimination.

Perhaps the most bitterly fought case to date is *Sobel v. Yeshiva University* (1988).[67] Judge Pratt of the Second Circuit Court of Appeals was persuaded by the plaintiffs' regression analysis on both counts of the disparate impact and disparate treatment theories, and he again remanded the case to the lower court, this time to a different trial judge.[68] The female medical faculty at Yeshiva used multiple regression analysis to show that during the pre-Title VII years (the pre-act years) the university's compensation policy had been discriminatory against the female faculty, creating disparate impact. After Title VII in 1972, the university still took no action to correct the disparities, hence maintaining the continuing effects of pre-Title VII discrimination.

While both parties agreed that experience, numbers of publication in scholarly journals, departmental affiliation, and faculty rank[69] are the relevant variables in the regression model, a bitter controversy developed over the use of the pre-act variable—the pre-act salary difference between male and female faculty members. Yeshiva contended that had the pre-act salary differences, for which the university could not be held liable under Title VII, been properly included in the model, the weight of the sex variable would have been reduced considerably, hence showing little discernable discrimination. The district court bought Yeshiva's argument in spite of *Bazemore*;[70] but Judge Pratt of the Second Circuit Court of

Appeals reversed it, holding that *Bazemore* required that employers equalize women's salaries immediately following the enactment of Title VII and that the pre-act salary differences, therefore, should properly be excluded from the regression model. In effect, the defendant employer could no longer "blame away" its pre-act discrimination. Pratt went a step further to conclude: "The failure to bring women's salaries up to par with those of men the day Title VII applied to Yeshiva is the sort of pattern and practice that would sustain a disparate treatment claim, even absent explicit proof of discriminatory motive."[71]

Technical complexities that are certainly not insurmountable abound in the use of multiple regression, such as the adequacy of the model, measurement and attendant assumptions, goodness of fit, and statistical significance.[72] In *Ottaviani v. State University of New York at New Paltz* (1988),[73] the university successfully refuted the plaintiff's regression analysis. In their orginal model the plaintiffs excluded the faculty rank variable from regression. They argued that academic ranks are in part a consequence of past discrimination and hence contaminated. To prove their points, the plaintiffs compiled descriptive statistics, and showed that New Paltz in the past had hired a disproportionate number of women into lower academic ranks. In its defense, the university took issue with that contention, and performed a separate regression analysis focusing on the initial assignment into ranks. The model included in the explanatory variables: (1) possession of a Ph.D., (2) publications, (3) years of prior college teaching, (4) years of related research experience, (5) years of other related experience, and (6) prior rank. The gender variable then was introduced to the equation to estimate the probability that a woman would be hired correctly into one of the four academic ranks. Regression showed that the model fitted well with the data, and that gender did not influence the assignment into initial rank.[74] *Ottaviani* is only a beginning. There will be many more such cases in future Title VII claims.

## CONCLUSION

Litigation, obviously, is not the only avenue by which to challenge the problem of pay inequity in employment. Legislation,[75] collective bargaining,[76] and making a different career choice (leaving gender-segregated occupations)[77] are other means to bring more equity into employment. This chapter focused on Title VII claims litigated in lower federal courts since the U.S. Supreme Court's landmark decision in *Gunther*. The survey of these cases suggests that writers and proponents for pay equity have overemphasized the importance of comparable worth, and they have unfortunately neglected the theory of intentional discrimination. Indeed, comparable worth claims for these years represented only a minor part—about 11 percent—of Title VII gender discrimination cases. When all but a few lower courts refused to recognize the comparable worth doctrine actionable under Title VII, and most recently when the Court of Appeals for the Ninth Circuit overturned a lower court's comparable worth ruling, many thought the final chapter had been written on comparable worth. It appears that Justice Rehnquist's dissenting view in *Gunther* has prevailed throughout in practice. Many feared that without comparable worth as a legal theory, the future of Title VII challenge to sex-based pay inequity claims would indeed be doomed.

Unexpectedly, however, *Bazemore* brought new life to Title VII challenges to gender discrimination. Where the *Gunther* Court left the contours of Title VII claims uncomfortably dangling, the *Bazemore* Court brought it to a closure by recognizing the viability of a multiple regression analysis. The decision provided a statistical methodology by which Title VII claimants may raise the presumption of intentional discrimination—the single most difficult task in Title VII litigation. In particular, a multiple regression analysis is found to fit well with the comparable work framework because it enables the plaintiff (as well as the defendant) to treat comparable positions or those similarly situated as though they are equal by systematically factoring out their differences. If comparable worth is a method of comparing apples and oranges, comparable work is analogous to a family of apples—not exactly equal, but not unacceptably different, either.

Based on the debate in *Gunther* one might surmise that Justice Rehnquist would have rejected comparable work just as he rejected comparable worth—as he wanted to see all gender-based wage discrimination claims strictly limited to the Equal Pay Act. Justice Brennan's formula, however, was open to other possibilities, although he never made that clear in *Gunther*. With *Bazemore* the Court has been able to change the equation significantly. Comparable work and multiple regression may be seen in this light, and *Denny*, *Sobel*, and *Ottaviani* may be a beginning to another chapter in the battle of gender in employment compensation.

## NOTES

1. Title VII of the Civil Rights Act of 1964, as amended in 1972, 42 U.S.C. Section 2000e-2(a)(1),(2) (1982).

2. *Spaulding v. University of Washington*, 740 F. 2d 686 (9th Cir. 1984).

3. *AFSCME v. State of Washington*, 770 F. 2d 1401 (9th Cir. 1985).

4. *County of Washington v. Gunther*, 452 U.S. 161 (1981).

5. Justice Rehnquist in dissenting view, *Gunther*, 181–204. Rehnquist rejected the comparable worth theory.

6. *Bazemore v. Friday*, 106 S. Ct. 3000 (1986).

7. The Equal Pay Act of 1963, 29 U.S.C. Section 206 (d)(1) (1982).

8. The Civil Rights Act of 1964, Title VII, Section 703(a)(1) and (h).

9. The term "authorized" became a focal point of controversy.

10. Section 206(d) of the Equal Pay Act states:

> No employer having employees subject to any provision of this section shall discriminate, within any establishment in which such employees are employed, between employees on the basis of sex by paying wages to employees in such establishment at a rate less than the rate at which he pays wages to employees of the opposite sex in such establishment for equal work on jobs the performance of which requires equal skill, effort, and responsibility, and which are performed under similar working conditions, except where such payment is made pursuant to (i) a seniority system; (ii) a merit system; (iii) a system which meaures earnings by quantity or quality of production; or (iv) a differential based on any other factor other than sex.

Part of Section 703(a) of Title VII, which was passed a year later in 1964 provides:

> It shall be an unlawful employment practice for any employer to fail or refuse to hire or to discharge any individual, or otherwise to discriminate against any individual with respect to his compensation, terms, conditions, or privileges of employment, because of such individual's race, color, religion, sex, or national origin.

Part of Section 703(h) of Title VII (the Bennett Amendment) attempts to connect the two statutes by providing (emphasis added):

> It shall *not* be an unlawful employment practice under the subchapter for any employer to differentiate upon the basis of sex in determining the amount of the wages or compensation paid or to be paid to employees of such employer *if such differentiation is authorized by the provisions of Section 206(d)* of (the Equal Pay Act of 1963).

11. *Gunther*, 171.

12. Ibid., 181.

13. *Gunther*, 203.

14. Ibid., 166.

15. Ibid., 181. Justice Brennan presumably left the determination of the legal contours to lower federal courts.

16. *Gunther*, 169 (this is Justice Brennan's view).

17. Ibid., 184 (this is Justice Rehnquist's view).

18. Ibid., 188.

19. Ibid., 190.

20. *McDonnell Douglas Corp. v. Green*, 411 U.S. 792 (1973).

21. *Texas Department of Community Affairs v. Burdine*, 450 U.S. 248 (1981).

22. If the plaintiffs are a class, rather than an individual, they must demonstrate that unlawful discrimination is the employer's standard operating procedure. See *International Brothers of Teamsters v. United States*, 431 U.S. 324, 360 (1977).

23. *Burdine*, 248.

24. *Griggs v. Duke Power*, 401 U.S. 424 (1971).

25. Jay M. Shafritz, Albert C. Hyde, and David H. Rosenbloom, *Personnel Management in Government*, 3d ed. (New York: Marcel Dekker, 1986). See especially "Equal Employment Opportunity," pp. 183–223.

26. See, for example, *Denny v. Westfield State College*, 669 F. Supp. 1146, 148 (D. Mass. 1987). See especially Footnote 1.

27. *AFSCME*.

28. Harold Suskin, ed., *Job Evaluation and Pay Administration in the Public Sector* (Chicago: International Personnel Management Association, 1977). See especially Appendix J: U.S. Government Primary Standard, pp. 640–651.

29. *American Nurses' Association v. State of Illinois*, 783 F. 2d 716 (7th Cir. 1986) provides an example of this inference.

30. The Equal Pay Act of 1963.

31. See, for example, *Miller v. Kansas Power & Light Co.*, 585 F. Supp. 1509 (1984); *Schulz v. Western Publishing Co.*, 609 F. Supp. 888 (D. Ill. 1985); and *EEOC v. Madison Community United School District*, 818 F. 2d 577 (7th Cir. 1987).

32. Thomas J. Campbell, "Regression Analysis in Title VII Cases: Minimum Standards, Comparable Worth, and Other Issues Where Law and Statistics Meet," *Stanford Law Review* 36 (July 1984), 1299–1324.

33. Ibid., 1320. See also *Spaulding*.

34. See *Penk v. Oregon State Board of Higher Education*, 816 F. 2d 456 (9th Cir. 1987); and *Sheehan v. Purolator Inc.*, 839 F. 2d 99 (2nd Cir. 1988).

35. *Spaulding*, 70.

36. See *Sobel v. Yeshiva University*, 656 F. Supp. 587 (S.D. N.Y. 1987); and *Denny*.

37. *Bazemore*.

38. Some cases were filed alleging more than one legal ground. The categorization in this table is based largely on the leading argument presented in court.

39. *Covington v. Southern Illinois University*, 816 F. 2d 317 (7th Cir. 1987).

40. See *Christensen v. State of Iowa*, 563 F. 2d 253 (8th Cir. 1977); *Lemons v. City and County of Denver*, 620 F. 2d 228 (10th Cir. 1980); and *AFSCME v. State of Washington*, 770 F. 2d 1401 (9th Cir. 1985).

41. *Spaulding*, 700.

42. 613 F. 2d 714 (9th Cir. 1981).

43. Ibid., 714.

44. Ibid., 697.

45. *AFSCME*, 1407.

46. See *Christensen v. State of Iowa*, 563 F. 2d 253 (8th Cir. 1977); *Lemons v. City and County of Denver*, 620 F.2d 228 (10th Cir. 1980); and *AFSCME*.

47. *Gerlach v. Michigan Bell*, 501 F. Supp 1300 (E.D. Mich 1980). See also *IUE v. Westinghouse Electric Corporation*, 631 F. 2d 1294 (3rd Cir. 1980); *Christensen*; and *Lemons*.

48. See *EEOC v. Hay Associates*, 545 F. Supp 1064 (E.D. Pa. 1982); and *Briggs v. City of Madison*, 536 F. Supp 435 (W.D. Wis. 1982).

49. *AFSCME*, 1404.

50. Ibid., p. 1406.

51. 673 F. Supp 893 (E.D. Mich. 1987).

52. Ibid., 902.

53. 783 F. 2d 716 (7th Cir. 1986).

54. Ibid., 726.

55. Ibid., 726.

56. U.S. Commission on Civil Rights, *Comparable Worth: An Analysis and Recommendations* (Washington, D.C.: Bureau of National Affairs, June 1984), 41–69. See also

Bill Shaw, "Comparable Worth and Its Prospects: *AFSCME v. State of Washington,*" *Labor Law Journal* 38 (Fall 1987), 100–118.

57. *Bazemore*, 3008.

58. The Equal Employment Opportunity Act of 1972 was an amendment to Title VII to make it applicable to public institutions.

59. *Bazemore*, 3009.

60. *Campbell*, 1323.

61. 505 F. Supp. 244 (1980).

62. 698 F. 2d 633 (4th Cir. 1983).

63. Ibid., 37. See also *Wilkins v. University of Houston*, 654 F. 2d 388 (5th Cir. 1981); *Segar v. Civiletti*, 508 F. Supp. 690 (FD. D.C. 1981); and *Trout v. Hidalgo*, 517 F. Supp. 873 (FD. D.C. 1981).

64. *Campbell*, 1302. See also Michael O. Finkelstein, "The Judicial Reception of Multiple Regression Studies in Race and Sex Discrimination Cases," *Columbia Law Review* 80 (1980), 737–754.

65. *AFSCME.*

66. 699 F. Supp. 1146 (D. Mass. 1987).

67. 839 F. 2d 18 (2nd Cir. 1988).

68. Female physicians on the faculty of the university's college of medicine brought sex discrimination charges against Yeshiva University, 572 F. Supp. 1509 (1983). The district court dismissed the complaint, and on appeal, the Second Circuit Court of Appeals in 1987 reversed the lower court holding and remanded for reconsideration in light of *Bazemore.* On remand, the district court again held against the plaintiffs for failure to establish a prima facie case of discrimination with respect to salary based on a multiple regression analysis. The physicians appealed once more.

69. The plaintiffs initially did not agree that the academic rank variable should be included in the regression equation.

70. Judge Pratt, obviously, was irritated by the fact that the trial judge failed to heed the circuit court instruction on remand. See *Sobel*, 37.

71. Ibid., 29.

72. *Campbell.*

73. 679 F. Supp. 288 (S.D. N.Y., 1988).

74. Ibid., 304. It was reported that "the probability that a woman would be hired correctly into: (1) one of the four ranks was 63 percent; (2) one of three ranks (combining professor and associate professor) was 87 percent; (3) the rank of instructor as opposed to the other three ranks was 44 percent; (4) an entry level rank as opposed to a nonentry level rank was 100 percent; and (5) the rank of instructor as opposed to assistant professor was from 44 to 80 percent.

75. Commonwealth of Virginia Secretaries of Administration and Finance, *A Report on the Status and Implications of Comparable Worth to the Governor and the General Assembly of Virginia*, House Document No. 3 (Richmond: Commonwealth of Virginia, 1985), 1–40.

76. Helen LaVan, Marsha Katz, Maura Malloy, and Peter Stonebraker, "Comparable Worth: A Comparison of Litigated Cases in the Public and Private Sectors," *Public Personnel Management* 16 (Fall 1987), 281–293.

77. Bureau of National Affairs, *Pay Equity and Comparable Worth, A BNA Special Report* (Washington, D.C.: Bureau of National Affairs, 1984).

## Appendix 6–A
## Pay Discrimination Claims Litigated in Federal District Courts from 1982 to 1988

| Federal District Court Cases | Equal Work | Comparable Worth | Comparable Work | Judgment |
|---|---|---|---|---|
| *Power* v. *Barry County*, 539 FS 721 (1982) | | X | | D.S. |
| *Briggs* v. *City of Madison*, 536 FS 435 (1982) | | X | | D.N. |
| *EEOC* v. *Hay Associates*, 545 FS 1064 (1982) | | | X | D.N. |
| *Langegan-Grimm* v. *Library Association*, 560 FS 486 (1983) | X | | | P.V. |
| *Connecticut State Employees* v. *Stte of Connecticut,* 31 Employment Practice 29,448 (1983) | | | X | P.V. |
| *Melani* v. *Board of Higher Education*, 31 Fair Empl. Prac. Case (BNA) 648 (1983) | | | X | P.V. |
| *Lewis* v. *Dekalb County*, 569 FS 11 (1983) | | | X | D.S. |
| *Craft* v. *Metromedia, Inc.*, 572 FS 868 (1983) | X | | | D.N. |
| *Wear* v. *Webb Co.*, 572 FS 1257 (1983) | X | | | D.N. |
| *Soble* v. *University of Maryland*, 572 FS 1509 (1983) | | | X | D.S. |
| *Shermnan* v. *City of Lee's Summit*, 577 FS 568 (1983) | X | | | D.N. |
| *AFSCME* v. *State of Washington*, 578 FS 846 (1983) | | X | | P.V. |
| *Miller* v. *Kansas Power & Light Co.*, 585 FS 1509 (1984) | X | | | P.V. |
| *EEOC* v. *Radio Montgomery, Inc.*, 588 FS 567 (1984) | X | | | P.V. |
| *Green* v. *Bettinger Co.*, 608 FS 35 (1984) | | | X | D.N. |
| *Minor* v. *Northvill Public Schools*, 605 FS 1185 (1985) | X | | | D.S. |

## Appendix 6–A, continued

| Federal District Court Cases | Equal Work | Comparable Worth | Comparable Work | Judgment |
|---|---|---|---|---|
| *American Nurses Association* v. *State of Illinois*, | | | | |
| No. 84 C 4451, Slip Opinion (1985) | | X | | D.S. |
| *Penk* v. *Oregon State Board of Higher Education*, | | | | |
| Civil No. 80-436 FR, Slip Opinion (February 1985) | | | X | D.N. |
| *Peng-Fei Chang* v. *University of Rhode Island*, | | | | |
| 606 FS 1161 (1985) | | | X | P.V. |
| *Schulz* v. *Western Publishing Co.*, 609 FS 888 (1985) | X | | | D.N. |
| *Koster* v. *Chase Manhattan Bank*, 609 FS 1191 (1985) | X | | | D.N. |
| *Horne* v. *Midland Corporation*, 613 FS 210 (1985) | X | | | D.S. |
| *EEOC* v. *State of Missouri*, 617 FS 1152 (1985) | X | | | P.V. |
| *Derouin* v. *Litton Industrial Products*, 618 FS 221 (1985) | X | | | D.N. |
| *Forsberg* v. *Pacific Northwest Bell*, 623 FS 117 (1985) | X | | | D.N. |
| *Heest* v. *McNeilab Inc.*, 624 FS 891 (1985) | | | X | P.V. |
| *EEOC* v. *Sears Roebuck*, 628 FS 1264 (1985) | | | X | D.N. |
| *Polay* v.*West Co.*, 629 FS 899 (1986) | X | | | P.V. |
| *Denny* v. *Westfield State College*, 669 FS 1146 (1987) | | | X | P.V. |
| *Monroe-Lord* v. *Hytche*, 668 FS 979 (1987) | X | | | D.N. |
| *AFSCME* v. *Nassau County*, 664 FS 64 (1987) | X | | | D.S. |
| *Selegson* v. *Massachusetts Institute of Technology*, | | | | |
| 677 FS 648 (1987) | X | | | D.S. |

**Appendix 6–A, continued**

| Federal District Court Cases | Equal Work | Comparable Worth | Comparable Work | Judgment |
|---|---|---|---|---|
| *Curtin* v. *Hadco Corporation*, 676 FS 408 (1987) | X | | | D.S. |
| *EEOC* v. *Altmeyer's Home Stores*, 672 FS 201 (1987) | X | | | D.N. |
| *International Union, U.A.W.* v. *State of Michigan*, | | | | |
| 673 FS 893 (1987) | | X | | D.S. |
| *Sobel* v. *Yeshiva University*, 656 FS 587 (1987) | | | X | D.N. |
| *Ottaviani* v. *State University of New York* | | | | |
| at *New Paltz*, 679 FS 288 (1988) | | | X | D.N. |

D.S. --Dismissed (no legal basis or on procedural ground);

D.N.--Denied (failed to persuade);

P.V.--Plaintiff prevailed in whole or in part.

**Appendix 6–B**
**Pay Discrimination Claims Litigated in Federal Courts of Appeals from 1981 to 1988**

| Federal Appellate Court Cases | Equal Work | Comparable Worth | Comparable Work | Judgment |
|---|---|---|---|---|
| *Padway* v. *Palches*, 665 F.2d 965 (1982) | | | X | D.S. |
| *Hall* v. *Ledex, Inc.*, 669 F.2d 397 (1982) | X | | | P.V. |
| *Standford Board of Education* v. *Standford education Association*, 697 F.2d 70 (1982) | X | | | P.V. |
| *Kouba* v. *All State Insurance Co.*, 691 F.2d 873 (1982) | X | | | D.S. |
| *Pelmer* v. *Parsons-Gilbane*, 713 F.2d 1127 (1983) | X | | | P.V. |
| *Stathos* v. *Bowden*, 728 F.2d 15 (1984) | X | | | P.V. |
| *Spaulding* v. *University of Washington*, 740 F.2d 686 (1984) | | | X | D.S. |
| *AFSCME* v. *State of Washington*, 770 F.2d 1401 (1985) | | X | | D.S. |
| *Foster* v. *Arcata Associates*, 772 F.2d 1453 (1985) | X | | | D.N. |
| *American Nurses' Association* v. *State of Illinois*, 783 F.2d 716 (1986) | | X | | D.S. |
| *Juanita Sellers* v. *Delgado College*, 781 F.2d 503 (1986) | X | | | D.N. |
| *Clark* v. *Terrant County*, 798 F.2d 736 (1986) | | | X | P.V. |
| *Marcoux* v. *State of Maine*, 797 F.2d 1100 (1986) | X | | | P.V. |
| *Gibbs* v. *Pierce County*, 785 F.2d 1396 (1986) | X | | | D.N. |
| *Covington* v. *Southern Illinois University*, 816 F.2D 317 (1987) | X | | | D.N. |
| *Penk* v. *Oregon State Board of Higher Education*, 816 F.2d 458 (1987) | | | X | D.S. |

## Appendix 6–B, continued

| Federal Appellate Court Cases | Equal Work | Comparable Worth | Comparable Work | Judgment |
|---|:---:|:---:|:---:|:---:|
| *Peters* v. *City of Shreveport*, 818 F.2d 1148 (1987) | X | | | D.S. |
| *EEOC* v. *Madison Community United School District*, 818 F.2d 577 (1987) | X | | | P.V. |
| *Feazell* v. *Tropicana Products*, 819 F.2d 1036 (1987) | X | | | D.S. |
| *Sellers* v. *Delgado Community College*, 839 F.2d (1988) | | | X | D.N. |
| *Sobel* v. *Yeshiva University*, 539 F.2d 18 (1988) | | | X | P.V. |
| *EEOC* v. *Sears Roebuck*, 839 F.2d 302 (1988) | X | | | D.N. |
| *Sheehan* v. *Purolator Inc.*, 839 F.2d 99 (1988) | | | X | D.N. |
| *EEOC* v. *J C Penney Co.*, 843 F.2d 249 (1988) | X | | | D.S. |
| *Pacific Northwest Bell* v. *Communications Workers of America*, 843 F.2d 1409 (1988) | X | | | D.S. |

D.S. --Dismissed (no legal basis or on procedural ground);
D.N.--Denied (failed to persuade);
P.V.--Plaintiff prevailed in whole or in part.

# 7

# *Immunities and Liability in Public Management*

In 1978, in *Monell v. New York City Department of Social Services*,[1] the U.S. Supreme Court reversed its 1961 decision in *Monroe v. Pape*[2] and declared that under the Civil Rights Act of 1871 (now codified as 42 U.S.C. Section 1983) local governmental bodies have no sovereign immunity protection from civil litigation initiated by injured parties. Two years later in 1980, first with *Owen v. City of Independence*,[3] then with *Maine v. Thiboutot*,[4] the Court went further to disallow even the qualified immunity from which local governments have received protection in civil litigation, holding them responsible not only for constitutional violations but for federal statutory violations as well. Additionally, the Court established that prevailing plaintiffs may recover attorneys fees from the defendant government.[5]

What the Supreme Court had done via *Monell*, *Owen*, and *Thiboutot* was to make a major policy shift on state and local governmental liability—not by legislation but by judicial interpretation.[6] Many feared that this policy shift might invite a flood of litigation against local governments[7] and public officials, thereby poisoning the administrative environment, creating disincentives for efficiency, and bringing a gradual erosion of cooperative federalism.[8] State and local administrators were understandably apprehensive about the expected rise of lawsuits and the attendant increase in insurance premiums.[9] Not everyone, however, shared this gloomy outlook. Others warned against overreaction, insisting that mechanisms are still built into our judicial system and local public administration that may mitigate the uncontrolled spread of lawsuits.[10]

This chapter summarizes the main shift in the federal liability law that governs local governments and their officials. Since neither the common law nor statutes have established that the federal and state governments have consented to be sued for the purpose of liability, it is appropriate at this time that attention be focused on governmental liability only at the local level. Insofar as the liability (or immunity) of governmental officials is concerned, as Rosenbloom[11] reported, there is a degree of interchangeability of the common law precedents between Section 1983 tort claims (against state and local officials) and constitutional tort claims (against federal officials).[12] Whereas official liability at the federal level flows directly from the Constitution (including the First, Fourth, Fifth, and Eighth Amendments), at the state and local levels it flows directly from the Civil Rights Act of 1981 (Section 1983) and state tort laws. In addition to identifying the shift in the law, this chapter explores the impact of the *Monell-Owen-Thiboutot* decisions on the state and local governments. In particular, it looks at the characteristics of damage suits, including litigants and the nature of their complaints, the likely targets of lawsuits, and the legal outcomes.

## BASIC CONCEPTS AND PRINCIPLES

Detailed case reviews on the subject of municipal liability have been extensively reported in various law journals[13] and in the public administration literature.[14] Here we summarize the main shifts in the law with respect to the authority and scope of the Civil Rights Act of 1871, now codified as 42 U.S.C. Section 1983.

### The Cause of Action

The doctrine of governmental immunity holds that government must consent to being sued; such consent offers a cause of action in court.[15] Following the passage of the Fourteenth Amendment, the Forty-Second Congress enacted the Civil Rights Act (CRA) of 1871 to control the Ku Klux Klan terrorism against newly emancipated black citizens. It was common knowledge then that the violence often was committed with the connivance of state and local government officials.[16] The relevant part of the CRA of 1871, now known as Section 1983, reads:

Every person who, under color of any statute, ordinance, regulation, custom, or usage, of any State or Territory, subjects, or causes to be subjected, any citizen of the United States or other person within the jurisdiction thereof to the deprivation of any rights, privileges, or immunities secured by the Constitution and laws, shall be liable to the party injured in an action at law, suit in equity, or other proper proceeding for redress.[17]

The question is whether Section 1983 represents governmental consent to suit. Curiously this provision was dormant for nearly a century until 1961 when a Mr. Monroe and his family, injured and humiliated by the city police but unable to recover relief under Section 1983, appealed their complaint to the U.S. Supreme Court. A lengthy review of the legislative history leading to the establishment of Section 1983 led the Court, for the first time, to rule that the section did not intend abrogation of the immunities of local governments. Central to the controversy was the phrase "every person" contained in Section 1983. The Court did not think that the phrase "every person" was meant to include municipalities.[18]

The *Monroe* controversy was revisited in 1978 in *Monell v. New York City Department of Social Services.* In *Monell*, several New York City female employees sued the city and other officials, complaining that the city's official policy forced pregnant employees to take unpaid leaves of absence even before medically necessary.[19] Four years earlier, in *Cleveland Board of Education v. LaFleur*, the Court had declared unconstitutional the board's policy setting arbitrary dates for unpaid maternity leave.[20] Applying *LaFleur*, the district court and the Court of Appeals for the Second Circuit both held against New York City, yet denied the plaintiffs relief, on the basis of *Monroe.* On certiorari, the Supreme Court examined the history again and said that the Court had made an error in *Monroe* and that the Forty-Second Congress did, indeed, provide a cause of action for constitutional injuries caused by municipalities. This represented a major shift in the law. What remained now were a few practical questions concerning the specific circumstances under which governmental entities and their officials (in person and in their official capacities) may or may not be held liable.[21]

In *Monell*, the Court dealt only with constitutionally protected rights, not with whether Section 1983 extends, as the phrase "and laws" in the statute suggests, to other statutory rights such as welfare and social security entitlements created by federal statutes. The Court resolved this issue in *Maine v. Thiboutot* in 1980,[22] where a class of welfare recipients attempted to recover lost welfare benefits plus attorneys' fees from the unlawful denial of AFDC (Aid to Families with Dependent Children) benefits. The Court held that Section 1983 created a cause of action for statutorily created rights as well as constitutionally protected ones. In Justice

Brennan's words, "Congress attached no modifiers to the phrase—'and laws.' "[23] Furthermore, the Court ruled that if the statutory action were properly brought under Section 1983, injured plaintiffs should be able to recover their attorneys fees under the Civil Rights Attorneys' Fees Awards Act of 1976, codified at 42 U.S.C. Section 1988. Attorneys fees often serve as a deterrent to plaintiffs bringing litigation.[24]

Does the phrase "every person" in Section 1983 extend to the states and their officials? *Monell*, which involved a local action, did not address this question, although it has been generally assumed that Section 1983 would not provide a cause of action against the states. It has been argued that Section 1983 would not supersede the Eleventh Amendment limiting the judicial power of the United States. The Eleventh Amendment declares, "The Judicial power of the United States shall not be construed to extend to any suit in law or equity, commenced or prosecuted against one of the United States by Citizens of another State, or by Citizens or Subjects of any Foreign State." In *Will v. Michigan Department of State Police*, 1009 S. Ct. 2304 (1989), the Court, in a narrow majority, concluded that the legislative history of Section 1983 does not lend support to the claim that the law represents the consent of the states to be sued. Likewise, Section 1983 would not provide a cause of action against state officials in their official capacity, because such suit would be a suit against the official's office. Section 1983, however, is construed to provide a cause of action against state officials in their personal capacity, since state officials are literally "persons" within the meaning of Section 1983.

### Absolute and Qualified Immunity

The common law has established that governmental officials at the local level (and at the state level in some cases) can be held liable not only officially but also personally for civil damages if such damages resulted from their illegal actions or misuse of power.[25] Absolute immunity is still preserved for judges, legislators, and prosecutors, for reasons of separation of powers or public policy—provided that their tortious action is taken within the limits of their duties and responsibilities. Only qualified immunity, however, is granted to policymakers in the executive branch when acting in good faith. The good faith immunity is also granted to those who are required to make discretionary judgments. In 1980, in *Owen v. City of Independence*,[26] the Supreme Court confirmed the existence of such immunities for governmental officials in their personal capacity, lest they should, in Justice Brennan's words, "exercise their discretion with undue timidity."[27]

With respect to local governmental entities, or governmental officials in their official capacity, the *Owen* Court disallowed the use of qualified immunity under any circumstance. Holding an official liable in his official capacity would be tantamount to holding his governmental entity liable insofar as compensatory damages are concerned. Considering both the history and purpose of public policy, the Court reasoned:

The central aim of the Civil Rights Act was to provide protection to those persons wronged by the "misuse of power," possessed by virtue of State law and made possible only because the wrongdoer is clothed with the authority of State law.[28]

Moreover, the Section 1983 was intended not only to provide compensation to the victims of past abuses, but to serve as a deterrent against future constitutional deprivations, as well. The knowledge that a municipality will be liable for all of its injurious conduct, whether committed in good faith or not, should create an incentive for officials who may harbor doubts about the lawfulness of their intended actions to err on the side of protecting citizens' constitutional rights. Furthermore, the threat that damages might be levied against the city may encourage those in a policy making position to institute internal rules and programs designed to minimize the likelihood of unintentional infringements on constitutional rights. Such procedures are particularly beneficial in preventing those "systemic" injuries that result not so much from the conduct of any single individual, but from the interactive behavior of several governmental officials, each of whom may be acting in good faith.[29]

Under *Owen*, it is now clear that local governmental entities have absolutely no immunity from monetary (compensatory) damages. In *Wood v. Strickland* (1975), however, the Court preserved absolute immunity for judges, prosecutors, and legislators (in their official capacity); it also preserved limited, qualified immunity for those in policy-making positions or whose duties require the use of discretion—insofar as their conduct does not violate "clearly established" statutory or constitutional rights of which "a reasonable person would have known."[30] This also applies to federal officials, pursuant to *Harlow v. Fitzgerald*.[31] While *Wood* addressed the immunity of state officials, *Harlow* focused on the immunity of federal officials. The Court in *Harlow* noted that "it would be untenable to draw a distinction for purposes of immunity law between suits brought against

State officials under Section 1983 and suits brought directly under the Constitution against federal officials."[32]

### Punitive Damages

If a purpose of the Civil Rights Act of 1871 was to serve as a deterrent to constitutional violations, should a local government additionally be held liable for punitive damages? The controversy arose in 1975 when the city of Newport, Rhode Island, failed to honor a contract with a rock concert group. In litigation, the U.S. District Court had imposed upon the city and seven of its officials a large sum of compensatory and punitive damages.[33] On appeal, the Supreme Court disagreed with the lower courts, in a six to three decision, arguing that the purpose of punitive damages is to punish the wrongdoer, not, by any means, to compensate the injured. Neither history nor logic, the Court contended, would justify punishing the tax-payers, precisely for whose protection the damages are imposed.

The importance of the *Newport City* rule cannot be overemphasized. As the Court acknowledged, the *Monell-Owen-Thiboutot* decisions already had expanded local governmental liability. What is worse—from the local government perspective—*Middlesex County Sewerage Authority v. National Sea Clammers Association*[34] had ruled that state and local governmental entities might possibly have to compensate persons harmed by abuses of governmental authority in a large range of administrative activity. Were punitive damages added to this, local governments would be at serious financial risk.[35] The *Newport City* rule, therefore, should be viewed as a measure of protection against lawsuits attempting to reach the "deep pockets" of government—liabilities extending to the level of the tax base.

The *Newport City* rule, however, does not apply to governmental officials in their personal capacity when actions have been taken in bad faith. What actions are considered as taken in bad faith (or not in good faith)? As the Court, in *Smith v. Wade*, discussed, the common law has distinguished between two types of bad faith actions, one acting in "ill will, spite, or intent to injure," and the other acting recklessly or in callous disregard of, or indifference to, the rights or safety of others. What standards (or threshold) has the Court provided for determining an official's personal liability—with regard to punitive damages? In *Smith v. Wade*,[36] the Court acknowledged, on the basis of state common law, that "punitive damages in tort cases may be awarded not only for action taken with actual intent to injure or in evil motive, but also for recklessness, serious indifference to or disregard for the rights of others, or even gross negligence." Concerning the latter, what if the official did not know about the existence of such rights? In *Wood v. Strickland*, the Court announced the standard: punitive damages may be awarded if the official "reasonably should have known" that the action he took within his sphere of official responsibility would violate the constitutional rights of the other.[37] In other words, lack of knowledge, in general, is no defense against punitive damages. As Rosenbloom argues, "In effect, the Supreme Court had made knowledge of constitutional law a matter of job competence for public administrators."[38]

## The Doctrine of Respondeat Superior

Respondeat superior liability means that, where an employer-employee relationship exists, the employer may be liable for the misconduct of its employees.[39] In *Monell*, the Court unambiguously rejected the respondeat superior theory,[40] pointing out that not only was the doctrine constitutionally untenable, but its application would be contrary to the spirit and language of Section 1983. Exploring the meaning of the employer's responsibiltiy (or liability) in this context, Justice Brennan focused on the phrase "shall subject or cause to be subjected" within Section 1983, and reasoned that:

> [T]hat language cannot be easily read to impose liability vicariously on governing bodies solely on the basis of the existence of an employer-employee relationship with a tortfeasor. Indeed, the fact that Congress did specifically provide that A's tort becomes B's liability if B "caused" A to subject another to a tort suggests that Congress did not intend Section 1983 liability to attach where such causation was absent.[41]

What this means is that a governmental entity or its officials may not be held vicariously liable for the misconduct of its employees unless a clear, affirmative link is present between the two in relation to the errant behavior. The concept of affirmative link was addressed earlier in *Rizzo v. Goode*,[42] which is now incorporated to *Monell*. In *Rizzo*, the mayor of Philadelphia, the police commissioner, and others were charged with the failure to control their police mistreatment of minority citizens. The Supreme Court reversed the lower court's judgment on the ground that no affirmative link had been established between the city's failure to take steps and the constitutional violations committed by the subordinate officials.[43] The affirmative link standard raises difficult questions of practical application. The causal connection may be clear, at least in logic, when an official or de factor policy or custom engenders constitutional violations; it can be quite problematic to attribute such nonactions as failure to act, inaction, negligence, or indifference as a causal agent of the constitutional or statutory injuries.

*Spriggs v. City of Chicago*[44] illustrates the complexity involved in respondeat superior doctrine. *Spriggs* sued the city of Chicago for monetary damages on the ground that the city's practice and custom, through its police officers, led to his injury. Spriggs presented evidence that the city was well aware of such police misconduct but failed to take steps to prevent or discourage such occurrences. To establish the affirmative link, the court evaluated Spriggs's allegation against the following four criteria: (a) whether the city had a de facto policy as evidenced by official inaction; (b) whether such inaction meant the failure to supervise where such control could be exercised; (c) whether the supervisor's inaction amounted to deliberate indifference or tacit authorization; and (d) whether the inaction or negligence was so severe as to be gross negligence or reckless disregard. The court found an affirmative answer to all but the last and, thereby, held against the city.[45]

To sum up the main point, it can be concluded that inasmuch as *Monell* created a cause of action against local governmental agencies and officers, it also placed potentially powerful constraints on the doctrine of respondeat superior, placing the burden directly on the plaintiff to show an affirmative link between governmental authority (e.g., policy, custom, or usage) and constitutional or statutory injury. The task may not be easy. When the *Newport City* rule—no punitive damages against governmental entities—is further incorporated to *Monell*, plaintiffs may not be able to recover damages without difficulty. It remains to be seen how the *Monell* dictum may evolve in practical applications.

## SECTION 1983 LITIGATION IN FEDERAL DISTRICT COURTS

How have *Monell*, *Thiboutot*, and *Owen* contributed to liability lawsuits? Have they invited increased lawsuits against state and local governments? Have they also contributed to the growth of Section 1983 lawsuits against government officials? Who are the litigants, and how successfully do they recover for their alleged damages? To obtain preliminary answers to these questions, this chapter examined a total of 1,709 lawsuits litigated in federal district courts from 1977 to 1983.[46] Note that 1977 was the year before the *Monell* decision was made; 1978 and 1980 were when *Monell*,

*Thiboutot*, and *Owen* were being made; and 1981 and 1983 were after these decisions went into effect.

## Lawsuits Against Government

When the Court overturned the *Monroe* decision in 1978, many feared that lawsuits against government would increase dramatically. Data show that between 1977 and 1983 there was a general and consistent increase in litigated lawsuits against all levels of state and local governments. The increase, however, was most serious for cities and counties, not for the states and school districts.[47] Whereas the states and school districts showed virtually no increase over the period, the lawsuits against the cities rose steadily from 46 in 1977 to 94 in 1983, and cases against counties rose from 4 to 32 in the same period.[48] This was expected. As discussed earlier, *Monell* provided a cause of action against municipalities, not the states, so that growth in litigation against the states should not have occurred. A growth in litigation against school districts was unlikely because the districts provide only limited public service. It is understandable, then, why an increase of lawsuits occurred primarily against cities and counties.

## Who Is Suing Government and Why?

Data (see Figure 7.1) also show that those who were litigating against government under Section 1983 were of six types: (a) individual citizens (621, or 37 percent); (b) public employees (442, or 26 percent); (c) prisoners (351, or 21 percent); businesses (126, or 7 percent); interest groups (83, or 5 percent); and welfare recipients (75, or 4 percent). As can be seen, three types of litigants—individual citizens, public employees, and prisoners—are responsible for the great bulk (83 percent) of Section 1983 lawsuits litigated in U.S. district courts.

This does not say, however, that *Monell, Thiboutot*, and *Owen* have had the most impact on these groups. The incidence of public employees' litigation or prisoners' litigation have not grown noticeably over the period under study. Nor has litigation increased by the recipients of public assistance including AFDC and the handicapped. The lawsuits litigated by this group remained about 5 percent. The difference, then, came mainly from litigation by individual citizens and business establishments. Between 1977 and 1983 the incidence of litigation by these two groups nearly doubled. Again, it can be said that *Monell, Thiboutot*, and *Owen* have had the most impact on individual citizens.

**Figure 7.1**
**Section 1983 Lawsuits by Types of Plaintiffs**

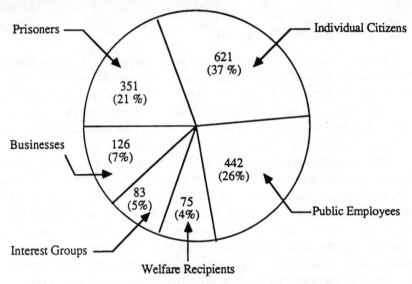

What were the sources of their complaints? Data (see Table 7.1) show that among the leading causes of litigation are the grievances occasioned by law enforcement, employment practices, application of due process rights in the conduct of public affairs (e.g., licensing), and enforcement of allegedly illegal statutes and ordinances. Collectively, these complaints made up approximately 85 percent of all Section 1983 lawsuits litigated in U.S. district courts. Lawsuits by individuals, which represent by far the largest category (about 37 percent), are largely based on due process violations (35 percent), police misconduct (about 30 percent), and grievances stemming from enforcement of constitutionally invalid laws and public policy (about 18 percent).

Complaints by public employees, which represent the next-largest category of litigants, are for the most part related to employment (about 83 percent) including discrimination on the job, employment termination, and refusal to renew employment contracts. A more detailed breakdown by occupational categories indicates that law enforcement and correctional officials are the most frequently litigating class (approximately 31 percent), followed by public school teachers with 30 percent, clerical and administrative personnel with 22 percent, and finally university professors with approximately 17 percent.

In the prisoners' case, most lawsuits seek general relief rather than compensatory damages, although some frivolous actions have sought multi-

**Table 7.1**
**Complaints by Types of Plaintiffs**

| Plaintiffs | Police Misconduct | Conditions of Confinement | Employment Practice | Due Process Violations | Denial of Benefits | Denial of Permits* | Invalid Statutes | Total |
|---|---|---|---|---|---|---|---|---|
| Individuals | 185 | 15 | 58 | 214 | 6 | 32 | 111 | 621 |
| Businesses | 11 | – | 5 | 26 | 1 | 21 | 62 | 126 |
| Public Employees | 8 | 2 | 375 | 26 | 5 | – | 26 | 442 |
| Welfare recipients | 1 | 1 | 2 | 3 | 55 | – | 13 | 75 |
| Prisoners | 39 | 112 | 3 | 153 | 2 | 25 | 15 | 349 |
| Interest groups | 3 | – | 10 | 15 | 1 | 2 | 50 | 81 |
| Total | 247 | 130 | 453 | 437 | 70 | 80 | 277 | 1,694 |

* Included in the permit category are licenses, business or project permits, and work release or parole.

million dollar damages. The chief causes of prisoners' lawsuits include various due process violations allegedly committed by prison officials (about 44 percent), complaints as to prison conditions (32 percent), and police brutality at the time of arrest (11 percent). The complaints by the recipients of public assistance are largely related to the denial of benefits (or entitlements) created by public law. Most business lawsuits are concentrated on such regulatory issues as permits, licensing, and business contracts.

### The Outcomes of Section 1983 Litigation

A lawsuit filed against a governmental entity or its officials is costly regardless of the outcome. But the financial burden can be serious when monetary damages are awarded against the entity or officials in their official capacity. General relief such as declaratory judgments, injunctions, and restraining orders may have long-term financial implications but their immediate financial consequences may be minimal or negligible. Understandably, therefore, monetary (or compensatory) damages have become the major concern of Section 1983 litigation.

To gain a perspective on litigation outcomes, we group judicial outcomes into three broad categories—general relief, monetary awards, and denial.[49] Data show an increase of cases in which monetary damages were awarded against local entities from five in 1977, the years immediately before *Monell*, to twenty in 1979, the year immediately after *Monell*, to twenty-nine in 1981, and then a drop to twenty-one in 1983. In terms of percentage of all cases litigated, there is no evidence of an increase, except for the first year following *Monell*. By contrast, lawsuits against government were dismissed at an increasing rate throughout the post-*Monell* period under study, for reasons other than sovereign immunity. These trends are unexpected, since *Monell* and *Owen* collectively established the policy of absolutely no immunities for local governments. The dismissal rate also holds true for cities. The observation is important, considering that cities have become the special target of Section 1983 litigation.

The dismissal rate also continues for governmental officials. Date show that as the courts denied or dismissed liability claims against officials at an increasing rate, in absolute numbers or in percentage, throughout the period studied, the incidience of officials held liable declined correspondingly. In 1977, in 155 out of 327 cases (about 35 percent), plaintiffs were able to prevail against government officials. By comparison in 1983, the plaintiffs prevailed in only 111 out of 439 cases or about 25 percent. Since *Owen* refused to allow even qualified immunity for local governmental entities, and thereby made it easier to hold officials liable in their official capacities, one would expect that the plaintiffs' prevailing rate would have been increased. Evidence, however, points to the contrary. An examination of seven years' data (1977–1983) seems to suggest that insofar as judicial outcomes are concerned, it is difficult to conclude what the precise impact of *Monell, Owen,* and *Thiboutot* has been on lawsuits against governmental entities and their officials.

## CONCLUDING OBSERVATION

The data presented in this study, and particularly the litigation outcomes discussed above, are puzzling. Why have the predictions of many failed to come true? Obviously some additional studies are needed. Within the context of this study, the null hypothesis demonstrated may not be too far out of line. First, Section 1983, as interpreted in *Monell,* does not override the Eleventh Amendment, so the *Monell* decision still provides no cause of action against the states directly. Where plaintiffs prevail against state officials, they still cannot recover damages if the money must come from the state treasury. This practice would definitely work as a disincentive to go after a state or its officials.

Second, although the Eleventh Amendment provides no constraints to a lawsuit against local governments, the judicial rules discussed in the review section might have provided a safeguard in the unmeritorious actions sought against local governments. The *Newport City* rule effectively bars the litigant from claiming punitive damages against governmental entities or officials where the money must be paid out of public coffers. Equally constraining is the substitution of the affirmative link requirement for the general doctrine of respondeat superior. As seen in *Spriggs,* the test for a causal connection cannot be met without genuine and persuasive argument. The review of these sample cases strongly suggests that it is not surprising that federal district judges often are weary of growing court filings seeking monetary awards from the public treasury. One district judge's comment is illuminating:

Civil case filings in this District during 1981 have once again followed the familiar pattern of breaking all previous annual records by a wide margin. As a concomitant to that increase without any corresponding increase in the number of judges, calendars grow even longer and more unmanageable. To some extent the increased influx is due to expanded sources of Federal jurisdiction. But all too much of this growth industry is traceable to "frivolous" actions (in the Federal sense) like Ragusa's negligence claims.[50]

Case data indicate that judges consider a significant number of cases to be outright frivolous. Not all judges, however, enter such judgments in their decisions, resulting in a sketchy impression at this time. One Missouri prisoner is known to have filed over five hundred complaints for litigation on his own behalf and now works in the prison as a writ writer for fellow inmates.[51] Against such background it may not be unreasonable to expect that the overcrowding of the court calendar especially by meritless or frivolous claims actually may encourage judges to be suspicious of civil claims and apply the rules more stringently. This may explain at least in part why the number of Section 1983 claims filed has increased somewhat as forecast but the number of successful claims has not increased significantly.

American public administration in the present century has seen a gradual demise of the sovereign immunity doctrine once so cherished by the old English Crown: "The King can do no wrong."[52] This evolutionary trend first occurred via legislation, both at the national and state levels, but it has been significantly reinforced by a series of decisions of the Supreme Court in the late 1970s and the early 1980s. The Civil Rights Act of 1871 (Section 1983) as interpreted in *Monell, Owen,* and *Thiboutot* represents the most important development in civil liability of local governments because in the federal system local governments are the hub of public service in which correspondingly most injuries can occur. Unique to the U.S. federal system, Section 1983 simply bypasses the Eleventh Amendment and *Dillon's* rule[53] to reach local governmental entities directly and make them responsible to the rights and privileges guaranteed by the Constitution and federal statutes. The private enforcement weapon in this case is monetary damages, punitive or compensatory. When the Supreme Court opened the door to civil litigation against local governments, some hailed the decision as a victory for liberal government, and others feared that the Court might just have opened a floodgate, especially to those who try to collect from the deep pocket of a government.

The impact of *Monell, Owen,* and *Thiboutot* could, and should, be examined from several perspectives, including all cases filed, not just the cases litigated, and other economic and psychological dimensions. In this chapter we have examined the cases actually litigated in federal district courts. The data show, among other things, that Section 1983 litigation has increased somewhat since *Monell,* but the increase has been confined mainly to cases against cities and counties. With regard to outcomes, however, it does not seem that the impact has been as pervasive as many feared. Even after *Monell,* federal district courts have continued to deny a high proportion of civil claims. Perhaps Steven Goode is correct[54] that several safeguards are built into the judicial system and public administration to prevent outright unreasonable lawsuits from spreading.

A caveat is in order. While the impact of *Monell, Owen,* and *Thiboutot* appears to be moderate in terms of litigation rates, the size of monetary awards may have an impact through increased insurance premiums and restricted coverage. Study is needed to understand the relationship between monetary awards and the rate of increase in insurance premiums.

This chapter suggests, among other things, that lawsuits by public employees, welfare recipients, and prisoners—although their combined incidence is high—are not a cause for alarm. The impact of *Monell* here appears to be minimal. The area of rapid growth in litigation that also seeks monetary damages involves individual citizens possibly wronged by local law enforcement and regulatory systems. The year 1986 witnessed a growth of insurance crises, in which municipalities were faced with huge increases in premiums—up to several hundred times—or worse yet, with restricted coverage, or in some cases, no coverage at all. To the extent that rising insurance premiums based on legal analysis poisons the environment of public management, a need exists to reexamine the reasonableness of the industry's database on which such calculations have been made.[55] But if a few categories of public service are capable of creating instances of civil injuries, thereby making the entire public system vulnerable to lawsuits, public administrators may have to reexamine the soundness of public policy dealing with public personnel systems. This can begin with analysis of recruitment policy, continued training and education, and proper supervision.

## NOTES

Several graduate students in the Department of Political Science at Iowa State University have assisted in developing the database for this study. My appreciation goes to Gerd Clabaugh, Bill Waller, Don Jegal, Chae-Young Jung, Won-Sok Lee, Dennis Martin, and Tim Jensen.

1. *Monell v. Department of Social Services of the City of New York,* 436 U.S. 658 (1978).
2. *Monroe v. Pape,* 65 U.S. 167 (1961).
3. *Owen v. City of Independence, Missouri,* 445 U.S. 622 (1980).
4. *Maine v. Thiboutot,* 448 U.S. 1 (1980).
5. Awards of attorney fees are based on the Civil Rights Attorneys' Fees Awards Act of 1976. What the *Thiboutot* decision did was incorporate this statute as an integral part of Section 1983 litigation. In most cases monetary awards for constitutional violations are nominal. It is quite customary that a court awards a nominal $1.00 for certain

constitutional violations, especially in prisoners' suits. Plaintiffs' attorney fees, however, may be quite expensive. See Appendix 7-A. One should also note that the attorneys fee provision may work against the plaintiff since attorneys fees can be awarded to the prevailing party, whether plaintiff or defendant. See *Bass v. Spitz*, 522 F. Supp. 1357 (1981).

6. W. Bartley Hildreth and Gerald J. Miller, "State and Local Officials and Their Personal Liability," in Jack Rabin and Don Dodd, eds., *State and Local Government Administration* (New York: Marcel Dekker, 1985), 245–264.

7. Robert H. Freilich, Jerusha L. White-Wasson, and Patricia K. Cofer, "1979–1980 Annual Review of Local Government Law: Municipal Liability," *Urban Lawyer* 29 (Fall 1980), 577–593. See also *Thiboutot*, 23 (Powell, dissenting).

8. Walter S. Groszyk, Jr. and Thomas J. Madden, "Managing Without Immunity: The Challenge for State and Local Government Officials in the 1980s," *Public Administration Review* 41 (March/April 1988), 268–278.

9. Eric Wisenthal, "Public Liability Woes Threaten Localities," *Public Administration Times* 8 (November 1, 1985), 1, 12; William F. Sueppel, et al., "The Deep Pocket Theory," *Iowa Municipalities* (July 1980), 10–12.

10. Steven Goode, "The Changing Nature of Local Government Liability Under Section 1983," *Urban Law Annual* 22 (1981), 71–104.

11. David H. Rosenbloom, "The Liability of Public Employees for 'Constitutional Torts,' " in Carolyn Ban and Norma M. Riccucci, eds., *Public Personnel Management* (New York: Longman, 1991), 129–142.

12. *Anderson v. Creighton*, 438 U.S. 635 (1987).

13. See Barbara Gilmore, "Case Notes," *Boston College Law Review* 23 (March 1982), 447–477; George D. Brown, "Whither Thiboutot? Section 1983, Private Enforcement, and the Damage Dilemma," *DePaul Law Review* 33 (Fall 1983), 31–74.

14. See David H. Rosenbloom, "Public Administrators' Official Immunity and the Supreme Court: Developments During the 1970s," *Public Administration Review* 40 (March/April 1980), 166–173; Charles R. Wise, "Suits Against Federal Employees for Constitutional Violations: A Search for Reasonableness," *Public Administration Review* 45 (November/December 1985), 845–856. See Groszyk and Madden, "Managing Without Immunity."

15. *Owen*, 649.

16. It was the common knowledge then that the violence often was committed with the connivance of state and local governmental officials. See Peter Schuck, *Suing Government* (New Haven: Yale University Press, 1983), 29–53.

17. 42 U.S.C. Section 1983 (Supp. III 1979).

18. *Monroe*, 187. The Court did, however, reverse the judgment of the lower court, acknowledging the Section 1983 liability against the police officers.

19. *Monell*.

20. *Cleveland Board of Education v. LaFleur*, 414 U.S. 632 (1974).

21. David O. Stewart, "The Supreme Court Rewrites a Law: Municipal Liability Under Section 1983," *The Urban Lawyer* 15 (Spring 1983), 503–513. See also Candace Cohn, "Municipal Liability Under Section 1983: The Failure to Act as Custom or Policy," *Wayne Law Review* 29 (Fall 1983), 1225–1244.

22. *Thiboutot*.

23. 42 U.S.C. Section 1983 (Supp. III 1979).

24. *Thiboutot*.

25. Clyde E. Jacobs, *The Eleventh Amendment and Sovereign Immunity* (Westport, Conn.: Greenwood Press, 1972). See especially chapter 5, "Suits Against Officers," 106–149.

26. In 1972, Richard Owen, stigmatized and discharged as chief of police without a name clearing hearing, filed his complaint against the city of Independence, Missouri, the city manager, and the city council. The district court held that Owen did not in fact have a property interest in his position as chief of police, as he was an employee at will, and it also held that his liberty interest had not been violated by the city. The Court of Appeals for the Eighth Circuit disagreed on the point of Owen's liberty interest and held that the Fourteenth Amendment provided Owen with a direct cause of action for monetary damages. The city petitioned the U.S. Supreme Court, believing that Section 1983 under *Monroe* immunized the local governmental entities from damage suits. Just before the Court might have granted the city certiorari, however, it decided *Monell*, and thus it remanded the case. On remand, the court of appeals applied the *Monell* rule and reaffirmed its earlier judgment, but it immunized all defendants, including the city, under the doctrine of qualified immunity, by consideration of the officials' good faith action. This time, Owen petitioned the Supreme Court for certiorari to obtain a ruling if a qualified immunity could be extended to municipalities for their good faith constitutional violations. The Court heard Owen's petition in 1980, just two months before *Thiboutot*. See *Owen v. City of Independence*, 589 F. 2d, 335 (1978).

27. *Owen*, 635.

28. Ibid., 650.

29. Ibid., 651–652.

30. *Wood v. Strickland*, 420 U.S. 308, 322 (1975).

31. *Harlow v. Fitzgerald*, 457 U.S. 800 (1982).

32. *Harlow*, 818.

33. *Fact Concerts, Inc. v. City of Newport*, 626 F. 2d 1067 (1976). Compensatory damages were in the amount of $72,910, and punitive damages were $275,000, of which $75,000 was to be spread among the seven individual officials personally and $200,000 against the city.

34. *Middlesex County Sewerage Authority v. National Sea Clammers Association*, 453 U.S. 1 (1981).

35. *City of Newport*, 279.

36. *Smith v. Wade*, 461 U.S. 30, 48 (1983).

37. *Wood v. Strickland*, 322.

38. Rosenbloom, "Liability of Public Employees," 136.

39. *Schuck*, 33.

40. *Monell*, 691.

41. Ibid., 692.

42. *Rizzo v. Goode*, 423 U.S. 363 (1976).

43. Ibid., 371.

44. *Spriggs v. City of Chicago*, 523 F. Supp. 138 (1981).

45. Ibid. Judge Getzendanner noted that a more relaxed standard has been used by some other judges. Ibid., note 7, p. 145. See also *DiGiovanni v. City of Philadelphia*, 531 F. Supp. 141 (1982).

46. The data for this study are identified from Federal Supplement reporters from 1977 to 1983 in every odd year. Data coded from the cases are the characteristics of plaintiffs and defendants, the nature of complaints, the court's determination on liability, and the types of relief, if any, granted.

47. For the purpose of this classification, towns and villages are included in the city category, and all special and school districts are classified into the school district category. Other administrative subdivisions such as transit and planning authorities are not included in the classification here. Although in a few instances these administrative subdivisions have been subject to lawsuits, the courts generally dismissed the complaints on the ground that they were not governmental entities within the meaning of Section 1983.

48. It may be noted that several lawsuits were litigated against municipalities in 1977, the year before the Court ruled in *Monell*. From case reviews we find that most Section 1983 claims prior to *Monell* had been either denied under *Monroe* or litigated directly under the Fourteenth Amendment in conjunction with 28 U.S.C. 1331, as permitted by the Supreme Court. See *City of Kenosha v. Bruno*, 412 U.S. 507 (1973). See the application of this rule in 444 F. Supp. 27 (1977). For discussion, see Groszyk and Madden, "Managing Without Immunity," 271.

49. General relief here refers to judgments without monetary awards, including declaratory relief, injunctive relief, and restraining orders. Included in the monetary award are compensatory damages, back pay, court costs, and attorneys fees where applicable. Denial means either dismissal or denial based on the failure to state a claim. Denials based on the statute of limitations or absention due to litigation at another jurisdiction are also included as part of the denial category.

50. *Ragusa v. Streator Police Department*, 530 F. Supp. 814 (1981).

51. *Green v. Camper*, 447 F. Supp. 758 (1978).

52. *Schuck*, 30.

53. John F. Dillon, Commentaries on the Law of Municipal Corporations, 5th ed. (Boston: Little Brown, 1911). The so-called Dillon's rule states that local governments are the creatures of the state.

54. *Goode*, 30.

55. George J. Church, "Sorry, Your Policy is Cancelled," *Time*, March 24, 1986, 16–26.

**Appendix 7–A**
**Some Examples of Dollar Amounts Awarded by Federal District Courts in Section 1983 Litigation Between 1977 and 1983**

| Year | No. of Cases | Average Dollar Amounts | Low | High |
|------|--------------|------------------------|-----|------|
| | | **Attorney Fees Awards** | | |
| 1977 | 7 | $ 11,783 | $500 | $27,760 |
| 1979 | 5 | 48,307 | 500 | 204,216 |
| 1981 | 26 | 20,902 | 500 | 82,350 |
| 1983 | 16 | 33,149 | 500 | 190,000 |
| | | **Court Costs** | | |
| 1977 | 4 | $2,427 | $65 | $3,558 |
| 1979 | 1 | 2,912 | 2,912 | 2,912 |
| 1981 | 8 | 2,443 | 132 | 12,384 |
| 1983 | 4 | 3,238 | 422 | 6,861 |
| | | **Monetary Awards** | | |
| 1977 | 6 | $48,552 | $75 | $200,000 |
| 1979 | 13 | 14,711 | 1 | 48,713 |
| 1981 | 21 | 63,031 | 1 | 564,000 |
| 1983 | 15 | 92,411 | 100 | 711,938 |

# 8

---

# *Implications for Management and Research*

We began this study by noting that during the past three decades, American public administration theory, particularly as it relates to personnel management, has undergone a fundamental shift with respect to the relationship between public employment and the Constitution. The purpose of this study has been to describe the emerging structure of this relationship and to explore the implications of this shift in the practice of public personnel management.

We pointed out that classical public administration theory pursued the value of efficiency (i.e., scientific rationality) as though it were almost an end in itself. To that end, classical writers had a vision of public administration that was centrally structured with the power vested exclusively in the executive. They believed that public employees could be organized as a politically neutral entity and that they could be made subject to the terms and conditions of the appointing authority. To them, constitutional provisions—particularly the First, Fifth, and Fourteenth Amendments—were largely inapplicable to public employees.

Many writers in recent years have faulted the classical formulation of public administration, pointing out that its underlying premise was at odds with the constitutional design of separation of powers. Moreover, classical administrative theory failed to describe the political nature of the administrative process in the United States.

Classical writers argued that Article II, Section 1 of the Constitution states, "The Executive Power shall be vested in a President of the United States." But they paid little attention to other places in Article I in which

the Constitution empowers Congress to share that administrative responsibility. Under this sharing arrangement, Congress is not only empowered
to create positions in the executive departments with the statutory authority
directly assigned to specific officials instead of to the President, but also
to appropriate funds, override presidential vetoes, and (in the case of the
Senate) confirm presidential appointees. From this perspective the critics
of classical public administration theory (or the politics of administration
school) were able to restructure the disciplinary inquiry grounded in
democratic administration emphasizing political accountability.

While the theory of democratic administration is closer to the design of
the Constitution than was the classical administrative framework, we have
argued that the politics of administration school did not go far enough insofar
as personnel administration is concerned. Note that the First Amendment of
the Constitution declares: "Congress shall make no law . . . abridging the
freedom of speech; or the press; or the right of the people peaceably to
assemble." And the Fifth and Fourteenth Amendments forbid the United
States or any state to "deprive any person of life, liberty, or property
without due process of law." Yet the politics of administration literature
paid little attention to the relationship between these constitutional provisions and public employment. Consequently, the politics of administration school, as in the classical efficiency school, contributed little to the
expansion of constitutional rights of public employees in the workplace,
let alone discrimination in employment, social inequity, sexual harassment, intrusions into privacy, restriction of basic freedoms, and misuse of
power. In some instances, public administration scholarship has given
advice that would legitimize the "imperial" administration.

According to Professor Richard Nathan, President Nixon attempted to
establish the "Administrative Presidency" in which public administration
is centrally coordinated and made exclusively loyal to the executive.[1] John
Erlichman's off-hand remark is an embarrassingly telling illustration of
the "Administrative Presidency." According to Professor Nathan, Erlichman, President Nixon's chief advisor for domestic council, is reported to
have said of the administration's new appointees, "when we say jump, they
will only ask how high?"[2] President Nixon and his top advisors might have
believed that the blind loyalty of public administrators was essential to get
control of public administration and to achieve the administration's policy
objectives. But the Constitution tolerates neither the blind loyalty of
administrators nor the centralized administrative structure.

On reflection, the idea of administrative presidency was not confined
to the Nixon administration. As scholars of American presidency would
agree, the activist presidents have all exhibited an ardor for the administra-

tive presidency. The administrative presidency, or what Professor Louis Koenig calls "the Sun King Complex,"[3] is a possibility under classical theory, as well as under the politics of administration school—as long as personnel administration is grounded not in the Constitution but elsewhere in the common law doctrine or the theory of political accountability. In either case, there is a danger that public employees can be mobilized as a machine (not as free men and women) to whatever cause some elected officials (or managers in the work unit) themselves may choose to define as a popular mandate. This type of concentration of power is precisely what James Madison sought to avert when drafting the Constitution. Madison wrote in Federalist No. 51:

> But the great security against a gradual concentration of the several powers in the same department consists in giving to those who administer each department the necessary constitutional means and personal motives to resist encroachments of the others. The provision for defense must in this, as in all other cases, be made commensurate to the danger of attack. Ambition must be made to counteract ambition. The interest of the man must be connected with the constitutional rights of the place. It may be a reflection on human nature that such devices should be necesary to control the abuses of government.[4]

As World War II came to an end and the nation became suddenly obsessed with loyalty and security concerns, the judiciary began to see a danger of power being concentrated in the administrative state—the power of the administrative state threatening the core of constitutional values: freedom, liberty, due process, and equal protection. At the heart of the power of the administrative state, as the Supreme Court saw it, was the common law doctrine of privilege that treats public employees as a special case separate from the constitutional framework. Upon reviewing a series of cases, the Court discarded the privilege doctrine as meaningless and constitutionally untenable. This opened the door to the constitutionalization of public employment.

In this book, we have taken a snapshot of the new public personnel environment grounded in constitutional values. Legal theories discussed and cases reviewed in this study are complex, yet the message is clear that the new environment is significantly different from the classical one that operated under the doctrines of privilege and political neutrality. The new environment expects that public administrators pursue efficiency (or organizational rationality) in a manner that is consistent with constitutional values. It rejects anticonstitutionalism in public employment—that is, expediency, discrimination, inequity, lack of due process, harassment, and restriction of constitutionally guaranteed freedoms. Instead, the new environment makes administrators obliged to respect others' constitutionally guaranteed freedoms, and requires that they be fair in managing personnel and that they not engage in, or cause, the deprivation of others' liberty and property interests without due process. As Professor John Rohr argued eloquently, all professional administrators take an oath to uphold the Constitution. "The oath to uphold the Constitution," Rohr wrote, "can then be seen not simply as a pledge to obey but also as an initiation into a community of disciplined discourse, aimed at discovering, renewing, adapting, and applying the fundamental principles that support our public order. The task is to see the oath more as an act of civility than submission."[5] The oath to uphold the Constitution also implies the right to disobey an unconstitutional order.[6] In the final analysis, the new environment demands that administrators improve their knowledge of the Constitution and keep abreast of case law.[7]

Compared with the classical administrative regime, the new environment presents challenges to administrators because case law is constantly in the making and administrators may not always be familiar with the constitutional implications of their action. In this regard, Justice Brennan's advice is particularly welcome. He advised that when officials have doubts about the lawfulness of their intended actions, "they had better err on the side of protecting citizens' [including employees'] constitutional rights."[8]

Some may argue that constitutionalism is good for individuals but bad for administrative efficiency. A danger, of course, exists that excessive legalism or constitutionalism may cause administrative timidity. But I would argue that a constitutionally competent administrator should be able to overcome that timidity because he or she would pursue a balance between efficiency and constitutionalism.

I believe that a democratic administration grounded in constitutional values promises the best of all possible alternatives. For one thing, constitutionalism does not negate the value of efficiency or administrative rationality. According to our unwritten constitutional heritage, efficiency is the axiom Number One, giving the raison d'être for public administration. In Justice White's words, "The essential rights of the First Amendment in some instances are subject to the elemental need for order without which the guarantees of civil rights to others would be a mockery."[9]

For another, constitutionalism should help increase efficiency. As we saw in the tragedy of the Watergate affair, President Nixon's administrative state wasted an enormous amount of national resources by attempting to undo the established constitutional order and later trying to cover its rear end. From the cases reviewed in this study, one can surmise without difficulty that litigated and unlitigated cases would be legion and that they all cost an unaccountable amount of public resources in defense of a runaway administrative state. In *Bazemore v. Friday* (1967), according to a local newspaper report, the state of North Carolina spent more than half a million dollars to prove why Mr. Bazemore and his Extension Service colleagues did not deserve a pay adjustment in compliance with Title VII.[10] Even with that, North Carolina lost the case. There are frivolous complaints, of course. But I contend that these incidences are minor. A reasonable alternative for an administrator is to take it seriously when an employee makes a complaint, formal or informal. This is because the Constitution creates a moral imperative that administrators pay attention to constitutional complaints—complaints that relate to a breach of constitutional values. From an efficiency point of view, too, it makes sense to address the problem at the early stage. Once a formal adversarial mechanism is set in motion, the cost is high in terms of time, energy, and money. Ultimately, the public suffers because their public servants are fighting for their own cause, and the administrative state is engrossed in its own defense. Adherence to constitutional values should help employees channel their energy to the service of higher ends.

On a positive side, constitutionalism should increase employee productivity because it inculcates a sense of equity in the workplace. The literature in human motivation provides evidence that inequity in the workplace destroys behavioral expectancy essential to human motivation.[11] The behavioral expectancy connects efforts to rewards, thereby steering energy to goal achievement. Inequity, discrimination, and mistreatment not only frustrate employee morale and productivity, but also dehumanize the work environment.

Constitutionalism also should promote creativity, because it unleashes human freedom—the freedom to be creative. Free men and women are, by definition, more creative than those in bondage. "On December 7, 1941," according to *USA Today*,[12] "Dorris Miller, a black man, stepped out of his place and took over a 'whites only' machine gun and blasted several Japanese warplanes from the sky. In manning that gun, Miller . . . became the first U.S. hero of World War II." The report continued, "Here was a black Navy messman who, despite being barred because of his race from even training to fire a machine gun, had outperformed white sailors who had received extensive training." Fifty years ago, it was the U.S. military's official policy that "blacks could not go to officers training school or flight school, operate radar or monitor sonar, navigate a ship or fire any of its guns. The only duties available for blacks in the Navy, in the service of their country, were literally positions of service—cooking food, waiting tables, making up beds, collecting laundry, cleaning toilets, shining shoes." Only by chance could Mr. Miller show his creative abilities to the service of his country that the military had denied to him.

Freedom encourages diversity in opinion and dissent, where necessary. The chances are greater that the ideals of our constitutional democracy will be realized when public employees are able to speak out on matters of public interest than when men and women of undivided loyalty do not ask questions even when they are asked to subvert the fundamental principles of our constitutional democracy.

Where do we go from here? It is high time that political science and public administration programs assert the primacy of constitutional values in their educational programs. The present situation is woefully inadequate. Many programs approved by the National Association of Schools of Public Affairs and Administration (NASPAA) do not require constitutional law or administrative law as part of their core curriculum. If future administrators, as Professor John Rohr envisioned, must be able to "think like judges, as well as like legislators and executives," the academics have responsibility to take the lead.

Public agencies and public administration professionals must develop a culture (ethics and norms) grounded in constitutional values. One cannot overemphasize the importance of organizational culture as it impacts on administrative behavior. All too frequently, constitutional injuries are inflicted on employees when those in positions of authority misuse their power under color of law. The problem for the injured party is compounded when the institution condones, and participates in, the coverup of the abusive behavior. The new public personnel environment makes it imperative that public agencies and administrators strive to develop a new culture promoting constitutionalism.

The Civil Service Reform Act of 1978 included the constitutional rights of employees among its nine merit principles. In recent years, professional societies, including the American Society for Public Administration, began to adopt a code of professional ethics safeguarding constitutional values. Many public agencies also have adopted a code of ethics for their employees. These are encouraging developments.

The paper work alone, however, is not sufficient. Inasmuch as public administration is the world of action, it must make a moral commitment to constitutional values. But public administration is more than the world of action; it is an academic discipline. As a discipline, it also must make a research commitment to measuring the progress toward the reign of a constitutional democracy.

## NOTES

1. Richard P. Nathan, *The Plot That Failed: Nixon and the Administrative Presidency* (New York: John Wiley and Sons, 1975).

2. Ibid., 81.

3. Louis W. Koenig, *The Chief Executive*, 5th ed. (New York: Harcourt Brace Jovanovich, 1986), 12.

4. Alexander Hamilton, James Madison, and John Jay, *The Federalist Papers* (New York: New American Library, 1961), 322.

5. John A. Rohr, *To Run a Constitution: The Legitimacy of the Administrative State* (Lawrence, Kan.: University of Kansas Press, 1986), 192.

6. Patricia W. Ingraham and David H. Rosenbloom, "The New Public Personnel and the New Public Service," *Public Administration Review* 49 (March/April 1989), 116–124. See also *Harley v. Schuylkill County*, 476 F. Supp. 191 (1979).

7. David H. Rosenbloom and James D. Carroll, *Toward Constitutional Competence: A Casebook for Public Administrators* (Englewood Cliffs, N.J.: Prentice Hall, 1990), 1–110.

8. *Owen v. City of Independence, Missouri*, 445 U.S. 622, 652 (1980).

9. *United Public Workers of America v. Mitchell*, 330 U.S. 75, 95 (1947).

10. *The Independent Weekly* October 9, 1989, 11.

11. David R. Hampton, Charles E. Summer, and Ross A. Webber, *Organizational Behavior and the Practice of Management*, 5th ed. (Glenview, Ill.: Scott, Foresman and Co. 1987), 18–21.

12. *USA Today* (December 3, 1991), p. 1.

# Appendix: Title VII of the Civil Rights Act of 1964

## SUBCHAPTER VI—EQUAL EMPLOYMENT OPPORTUNITIES

### § 2000e. Definitions

For the purposes of this subchapter—

(a) The term "person" includes one or more individuals, governments, governmental agencies, political subdivisions, labor unions, partnerships, associations, corporations, legal representatives, mutual companies, joint-stock companies, trusts, unincorporated organizations, trustees, trustees in cases under title 11, or receivers.

(b) The term "employer" means a person engaged in an industry affecting commerce who has fifteen or more employees for each working day in each of twenty or more calendar weeks in the current or preceding calendar year, and any agent of such a person, but such term does not include (1) the United States, a corporation wholly owned by the Government of the United States, an Indian tribe, or any department or agency of the District of Columbia subject by statute to procedures of the competitive service (as defined in section 2102 of title 5), or (2) a bona fide private membership club (other than a labor organization) which is exempt from taxation under section 501(c) of title 26, except that during the first year after March 24, 1972, persons having fewer than twenty-five employees (and their agents) shall not be considered employers.

(c) The term "employment agency" means any person regularly undertaking with or without compensation to procure employees for an employer or to procure for employees opportunities to work for an employer and includes an agent of such a person.

(d) The term "labor organization" means a labor organization engaged in an industry affecting commerce, and any agent of such an organization, and includes any organization of any kind, any agency, or employee representation committee, group, association, or plan so engaged in which employees participate and which exists for the purpose, in whole or in part, of dealing with employers concerning grievances, labor disputes, wages, rates of pay, hours, or other terms or conditions of employment, and any conference, general committee, joint or system board, or joint council so engaged which is subordinate to a national or international labor organization.

(e) A labor organization shall be deemed to be engaged in an industry affecting commerce if (1) it maintains or operates a hiring hall or hiring office which procures employees for an employer or procures for employees opportunities to work for an employer, or (2) the number of its members (or, where it is a labor organization composed of other labor organizations or their representatives, if the aggregate number of the members of such other labor organization) is (A) twenty-five or more during the first year after March 24, 1972, or (B) fifteen or more thereafter, and such labor organization—

(1) is the certified representative of employees under the provisions of the National Labor Relations Act, as amended [29 U.S.C. 151 et seq.] or the Railway Labor Act, as amended [45 U.S.C. 151 et seq.];

(2) although not certified, is a national or international labor organization or a local labor organization recognized or acting as the representative of employees of an employer or employers engaged in an industry affecting commerce; or

(3) has chartered a local labor organization or subsidiary body which is representing or actively seeking to represent employees of employers within the meaning of paragraph (1) or (2); or

(4) has been chartered by a labor organization representing or actively seeking to represent employees within the meaning of paragraph (1) or (2) as the local or subordinate body through which such employees may enjoy membership or become affiliated with such labor organization; or

(5) is a conference, general committee, joint or system board, or joint council subordinate to a national or international labor organization, which includes a labor organization engaged in an industry affecting commerce within the meaning of any of the preceding paragraphs of this subsection.

(f) The term "employee" means an individual employed by an employer, except that the term "employee" shall not include any person elected to public office in any State or political subdivision of any State by the qualified voters thereof, or any person chosen by such officer to be on such officer's personal staff, or an appointee on the policy making level or an immediate adviser with respect to the exercise of the constitutional or legal powers of the office. The exemption set forth in the preceding sentence shall not include employees subject to the civil service laws of a State government, governmental agency or political subdivision.

(g) The term "commerce" means trade, traffic, commerce, transportation, transmission, or communication among the several States; or between a State and any place outside thereof; or within the District of Columbia, or a possesion of the United States; or between points in the same State but through a point outside thereof.

(h) The term "industry affecting commerce" means any activity, business, or industry in commerce or in which a labor dispute would hinder or obstruct commerce or the free flow of commerce and includes any activity or industry "affecting commerce" within the meaning of the Labor-Management Reporting and Disclosure Act of 1959 [29 U.S.C. 401 et seq.], and further includes any governmental industry, business, or activity.

(i) The term "State" includes a State of the United States, the District of Columbia, Puerto Rico, the Virgin Islands, American Samoa, Guam, Wake Island, the Canal Zone, and Outer Continental Shelf lands defined in the Outer Continental Shelf Lands Act [43 U.S.C. 1331 et seq.].

(j) The term "religion" includes all aspects of religious observance and practice, as well as belief, unless an employer demonstrates that he is unable to reasonably accommodate to an employee's or prospective employee's religious observance or practice without undue hardship on the conduct of the employer's business.

(k) The terms "because of sex" or "on the basis of sex" include, but are not limited to, because of or on the basis of pregnancy, childbirth, or related medical conditions; and women affected by pregnancy, childbirth, or related medical conditions shall be treated the same for all employment-related purposes, including receipt of benefits under fringe benefit programs, as other persons not so affected but similar in their ability or inability to work, and nothing in section 2000e–2(h) of this title shall be interpreted to permit otherwise. This subsection shall not require an employer to pay for health insurance benefits for abortion, except where the life of the mother would be endangered if the fetus were carried to term, or except where medical complications have arisen from an abortion: *Provided*, That nothing herein shall preclude an employer from providing abortion benefits or otherwise affect bargaining agreements in regard to abortion.

### § 2000e–2. Unlawful employment practices

#### (a) Employer practices

It shall be an unlawful employment practice for an employer—

(1) to fail or refuse to hire or to discharge any individual, or otherwise to discriminate against any individual with respect to his compensation, terms, conditions, or privileges of employment, because of such individual's race, color, religion, sex, or national origin; or

(2) to limit, segregate, or classify his employees or applicants for employment in any way which would deprive or tend to deprive any individual of employment opportunities or otherwise adversely affect his status as an employee, because of such individual's race, color, religion, sex, or national origin.

#### (b) Employment agency practices

It shall be an unlawful employment practice for an employment agency to fail or refuse to refer for employment, or otherwise to discriminate against, any individual because of his race, color, religion, sex, or national origin, or to classify or refer for employment any individual on the basis of his race, color, religion, sex, or national origin.

#### (c) Labor organization practices

It shall be an unlawful employment practice for a labor organization—

(1) to exclude or to expel from its membership, or otherwise to discriminate against, any individual because of his race, color, religion, sex, or national origin;

(2) to limit, segregate, or classify its membership or applicants for membership, or to classify or fail or refuse to refer for employment any individual, in any way which would deprive or tend to deprive any individual of employment opportunities, or would limit such employment opportunities or otherwise adversely affect his status as an employee or as an applicant for employment, because of such individual's race, color, religion, sex, or national origin; or

(3) to cause or attempt to cause an employer to discriminate against an individual in violation of this section.

### (d) Training programs

It shall be an unlawful employment practice for any employer, labor organization, or joint labor-management committee controlling apprenticeship or other training or retraining, including on-the-job training programs to discriminate against any individual because of his race, color, religion, sex, or national origin in admission to, or employment in, any program established to provide apprenticeship or other training.

### (e) Businesses or enterprises with personnel qualified on basis of religion, sex, or national origin; educational institutions with personnel of particular religion

Notwithstanding any other provision of this subchapter, (1) it shall not be an unlawful employment practice for an employer to hire and employ employees, for an employment agency to classify, or refer for employment any individual, for a labor organization to classify its membership or to classify or refer for employment any individual, or for an employer, labor organization, or joint labor-management committee controlling apprenticeship or other training or retraining programs to admit or employ any individual in any such program, on the basis of his religion, sex, or national origin in those certain instances where religion, sex, or national origin is a bona fide occupational qualification reasonably necessary to the normal operation of that particular business or enterprise, and (2) it shall not be an unlawful employment practice for a school, college, university, or other educational institution or institution of learning to hire and employ employees of a particular religion if such school, college, university, or other educational institution or institution of learning is, in whole or in substantial part, owned, supported, controlled, or managed by a particular religion or by a particular religious corporation, association, or society, or if the curriculum of such school, college, university, or other educational institution or institution of learning is directed toward the propagation of a particular religion.

### (f) Members of Communist Party or Commuinist-action or Communist-front organizations

As used in this subchapter, the phrase "unlajwful employment practice" shall not be deemed to include any action or measure taken by an employer, labor organization, joint labor-management committee, or employment agency with respect to an individual who is a member of the Communist Party of the United States or of any other organization required to register as a Communist-action or Communist-front organization by final order of the Subversive Activities Control Board pursuant to the Subversive Activities Control Act of 1950 [50 U.S.C. 781 et seq.].

### (g) National security

Notwithstanding any other provision of this subchapter, it shall not be an unlawful employment practice for an employer to fail or refuse to hire and employ any individual for any position, for an employer to discharge any individual from any position, or for an employment agency to fail or refuse to refer any individual for employment in any position, or for a labor organization to fail or refuse to refer any individual for employment in any position, if—

(1) the occupancy of such position, or access to the premises in or upon which any part of the duties of such position is performed or is to be performed, is subject to any requirement imposed in the interest of the national security of the United States under any security program in effect pursuant to or administered under any statute of the United States or any Executive order of the President; and

(2) such individual has not fulfilled or has ceased to fulfill that requirement.

**(h) Seniority or merit system; quantity or quality of production; ability tests; compensation based on sex and authorized by minimum wage provisions**

Notwithstanding any other provision of this subchapter, it shall not be an unlawful employment practice for an employer to apply different standards of compensation, or different terms, conditions, or privileges of employment pursuant to a bona fide seniority or merit system, or a system which measures earnings by quantity or quality of production or to employees who work in different locations, provided that such differences are not the result of an intention to discriminate because of race, color, religion, sex, or national origin, nor shall it be an unlawful employment practice for an employer to give and to act upon the results of any professionally developed ability test provided that such test, its administration or action upon the results is not designed, intended or used to discriminate because of race, color, religion, sex or national origin. It shall not be an unlawful employment practice under this subchapter for any employer to differentiate upon the basis of sex in determining the amount of the wages or compensation paid or to be paid to employees of such employer if such differentiation is authorized by the provisions of section 206(d) of title 29.

**(i) Businesses or enterprises extending preferential treatment to Indians**

Nothing contained in this subchapter shall apply to any business or enterprise on or near an Indian reservation with respect to any publicly announced employment practice of such business or enterprise under which a preferential treatment is given to any individual because he is an Indian living on or near a reservation.

**(j) Preferential treatment not to be granted on account of existing number or percentage imbalance**

Nothing contained in this subchapter shall be interpreted to require any employer, employment agency, labor organization, or joint labor-management committee subject to this subchapter to grant preferential treatment to any individual or to any group because of the race, color, religion, sex, or national origin of such individual or group on account of an imbalance which may exist with respect to the total number or percentage of persons of any race, color, religion, sex, or national origin employed by any employer, referred or classified for employment by any employment agency or labor organization, admitted to membership or classified by any labor organization, or admitted to, or employed in, any apprenticeship or other training program, in comparison with the total number or percentage of persons of such race, color, religion, sex, or national origin in any community, State, section, or other area, or in the available work force in any community, State, section, or other area.

# Selected Bibliography

Ban, Carolyn, and Norma M. Riccucci, eds. *Public Personnel Management*. New York: Longman, 1991.

Baum, Lawrence. *The Supreme Court*. 3rd ed. Washington, D.C.: Congressional Quarterly Inc., 1989.

Brownlow, Louis, Charles E. Merriam, & Luther Gulick. *Administrative Management in the Government of the United States: A Report of the President's Committee on Administrative Management*. Washington, D.C.: U.S. Government Printing Office, 1937.

Bureau of National Affairs. *Pay Equity and Comparable Worth: ABNA Special Report*. Washington, D.C.: Bureau of National Affairs, 1984.

Campbell, Alan K. "Civil Service Reform: A New Commitment." *Public Administration Review* 38 (March/April 1978), 99–103.

Campbell, Thomas J. "Regression Analysis in Title VII Cases: Minimum Standards, Comparable Worth and Other Issues Where Law and Statistics Meet." *Stanford Law Review* 36 (July 1984), 1299–1324.

Cooper, Phillip J. *Public Law and Public Administration*. 2nd ed. Englewood Cliffs, N.J.: Prentice Hall, 1988.

Couturier, Jean J. "The Quiet Revolution in Public Personnel Laws." *Public Personnel Management* (May/June 1976).

Dimock, Marshall E. "The Study of Administration." *American Political Science Review* 31 (February 1937), 28–40.

Dotson, Arch. "The Emerging Doctrine of Privilege in Public Employment." *Public Administration Review* 15, no. 2 (Spring 1955): 77–88.

Dresang, Dennis L. *Public Personnel Management and Public Policy*. Boston: Little, Brown and Co., 1984.

Equal Employment Opportunity Commission. "Uniform Guidelines on Employee Selection Procedures." *Federal Register* 43: 166 (Friday, August 25, 1978).

Finer, Herman. "Administrative Responsibility in Democratic Government." *Public Administration Review* 1 (1941), 335–350.

Gawthrop, Louis C., ed. *The Administrative Process and Democratic Theory.* New York: Houghton Mifflin, 1970.

Geel, T. R. Van. (1991) *Understanding Supreme Court Opinions.* New York: Longman, 1991.

Goldman, Alan H. *Justice and Reverse Discrimination.* Princeton: Princeton University Press, 1979.

Goldman, Deborah D. "Due Process and Public Personnel Management." *Review of Public Personnel Administration* 2 (Fall 1981), 19–27.

Goodnow, Frank J. *Politics and Administration: A Study in Government.* New York: Macmillan, 1990.

Groszyk, Walter S. Jr., and Thomas J. Madden. "Managing Without Immunity: The Challenge for State and Local Government Officials in the 1980s." *Public Administration Review* 41 (March/April 1985), 268–278.

Gulick, Luther, and L. Urwick, eds. *Papers on the Science of Administration.* New York: Columbia University Press, 1937.

Hamilton, Alexander, James Madison, and John Jay. *The Federalist Papers.* New York: New American Library, 1961.

Hampton, David R., Charles E. Summer, and Ross A. Webber. *Organizational Behavior and the Practice of Management.* 5th ed. Glenview, Ill: Scott, Foresman and Co., 1987.

Hays, Steven W., and Richard C. Kerney, eds. *Public Personnel Administration.* Englewood Cliffs, N.J.: Prentice Hall, 1990.

Hildreth, W. Bartley, and Gerald Miller, "State and Local Officials and their Personal Liability," in Jack Robin and Don Dodd, eds., *State and Local Administration* (New York: Marcel Dekker, 1985), 245–264.

Hunt, James W. *The Law of the Workplace.* Washington, D.C.: Bureau of National Affairs, 1984.

Ingraham, Patricia W., and David H. Rosenbloom. "The New Public Personnel and the New Public Service." *Public Administration Review* 49 (March/April 1989), 116–124.

Jacobs, Clyde E. *The Eleventh Amendment and Sovereign Immunity.* Westport, Conn.: Greenwood Press, 1972.

Kaufman, Herbert. "Emerging Conflicts in the Doctrine of Public Administration." *American Political Science Review* 50 (December 1956), 1057–1073.

Klingner, Donald E. *Public Personnel Management: Context and Strategies.* Englewood, Cliffs, N.J.: Prentice Hall, 1980.

Krislov, Samuel. *The Negro in Federal Employment.* Minneapolis: University of Minnesota Press, 1967.

Koenig, Louis W. *The Chief Executive.* 5th ed. New York: Harcourt Brace Jovanovich, 1986.

Lee, Robert D., Jr. *Public Personnel Systems.* Rockville, Md.: Aspen Publishers, 1987.

Lee, Yong S. "Civil Liability of State and Local Government." *Public Administration Review* 47, no. 2 (March/April 1987): 160–170.

———. "Shaping Judicial Response to Gender Discrimination in Employment Compensation." *Public Administration Review* 49, no. 5 (September/October 1989), 420–430.

————— . "Affirmative Action and Judicial Standards of Review." *Review of Public Personnel Administration* 12 (Spring 1992).

Lewis, Anthony. *Make No Law.* New York: Random House, 1991.

Lockhard, Duane, and Walter F. Murphy. (1992) *Basic Cases in Constitutional Law.* 3rd ed. Washington, D.C.: Congressional Quarterly Inc., 1992.

Long, Norton E. "Bureaucracy and Constitutionalism." *American Political Science Review* 46 (September 1952), 808–818.

Louthan, Williams C. *The United States Supreme Court.* Englewood Cliffs, N.J.: Prentice Hall, 1991.

Lowi, Theodore J. *The End of Liberalism.* New York: W. W. Norton & Co., 1969.

Meier, Kenneth. "Representative Bureaucracy: An Empirical Analysis." *American Political Science Review* 69 (1975).

Mosher, Frederick C. *Democracy and the Public Service.* New York: Oxford University Press, 1968.

Nalbandian, John. "The U.S. Supreme Court's 'Consensus' on Affirmative Action." *Public Administration Review* 49 (January/February 1989), 38–45.

Nathan, Richard P. *The Plot That Failed: Nixon and the Administrative Presidency.* New York: John Wiley and Sons, 1975.

National Commission on the Public Service. *Leadership for America: Rebuilding the Public Service.* Washington, D.C.: Government Printing Office, 1989.

Newland, Chester A. "Public Personnel Administration: Legalistic Reforms v. Effectiveness, Efficiency, and Economy." *Public Administration Review* 36 (September/October 1976).

Ostrom, Vincent. *The Intellectual Crisis in American Public Administration.* University of Alabama Press, 1973.

Ostrom, Vincent, and Elinor Ostrom. "Public Choice: A Different Approach to the Study of Public Administration." *Public Administration Review* 31 (March/April 1971).

Rabin, Jack, and Don Dodd, eds. *State and Local Government Administration.* New York: Marcel Dekker, 1985.

Rice, Mitchell F. "Government Set-Asides, Minority Business Enterprises, and the Supreme Court." *Public Administration Review* 51 (March/April 1991), 114–122.

Rohr, John A. *Ethics for Bureaucrats.* New York: Marcel Dekker, 1978.

————— . *To Run a Constitution: The Legitimacy of the Administrative State.* Lawrence, Kan.: University of Kansas Press, 1986.

Rosenbloom, David H. *Federal Service and the Constitution.* Ithaca, N.Y.: Cornell University Press, 1971.

————— . "Public Personnel Administration and the Constitution: An Emergent Approach." *Public Administration Review* 35, no. 1 (January/February 1975).

————— . *Public Personnel Administration and Law.* New York: Marcel Dekker, 1983.

————— . "Public Administrators and the Judiciary: The 'New Partnership.' " *Public Administration Review* 47 (January/February 1987): 75–83.

————— . "The Public Employment Relationship and the Supreme Court in the 1980s." *Review of Public Personnel Administration* 8 (Spring 1988).

Rosenbloom, David H., and James D. Carroll. *Toward Constitutional Competence: A Casebook for Public Administrators.* Englewood Cliffs, N.J.: Prentice Hall, 1990.

Rourke, Francis E., ed. *Bureaucratic Power in National Policy Making*. 4th ed. Boston: Little, Brown and Co., 1986.

Sayre, Wallace. "The Triumph of Techniques Over Purpose." *Public Administration Review* 8 (Spring 1948).

Shafritz, Jay M., Albert C. Hyde, and David H. Rosenbloom. *Personnel Management in Government*. 3rd ed. New York: Marcel Dekker, 1986.

Shafritz, Jay M., and Albert C. Hyde, eds. *Classics of Public Administration*. 2nd ed. Pacific Grove, Calif.: Brooks/Cole Publishing Co., 1987.

Simon, Herbert. *Administrative Behavior*. New York: The Free Press, 1947.

Stewart, David O. "The Supreme Court Rewrites a Law: Municipal Liability Under Section 1983." *The Urban Lawyer* 15 (Spring 1983), 503–513.

Suskin, Harold, ed. *Job Evaluation and Pay Administration in the Public Sector*. Chicago: International Personnel Management Association, 1977.

Sylvia, Ronald D. *Critical Issues in Public Personnel Policy*. Pacific Grove, Calif.: Brooks/Cole Publishing Co., 1989.

Thompson, Frank J., ed. *Classics of Public Personnel Policy*. 2nd ed. Pacific Grove, Calif.: Brooks/Cole Publishing Co., 1991.

U.S. Commission on Civil Rights. *Comparable Worth: An Analysis and Recommendations*. Washington, D.C.: Bureau of National Affairs, 1984.

U.S. Merit Systems Protection Board. *Federal Personnel Policies and Practices: Perspectives from the Workplace*. Washington, D.C.: USMSPB, 1987.

Van Riper, Paul P. *History of the United States Civil Service*. Evanston, Ill.: Row, Peterson, 1958.

Waldo, Dwight. *The Study of Public Administration*. New York: Random House, 1955.

White, Leonard. *Introduction to the Study of Public Administration*. New York: Macmillan, 1939.

Wilson, Woodrow. "The Study of Administration." *Political Science Quarterly* 2 (June 1887): 198–222.

# Index

## ABOUT THE AUTHOR

YONG S. LEE is Associate Professor of Political Science at Iowa State University. He is a widely published author of articles in such journals as *Public Administration Review, Review of Public Personnel Administration, Journal of Human Resources Administration,* and *Journal of Management Science and Policy Analysis.*